Rachel Allen

Home Baking

Rachel Allen
Home Baking

HarperCollins*Publishers*

Contents

Introduction

Baking has long been a source of joy and comfort in my life. I have vivid early memories of impatiently waiting alongside my mum and sister for sweet treats to emerge from the oven, and I've never tired of that wonderful sense of anticipation. For me, baking is a moment of respite and some time for contemplation. But it's also time spent bustling around the kitchen with my family and friends. Either way, I think there's something so joyous about stirring, kneading or whipping together ingredients and waiting (not always patiently) for the end result. I find the aromas, textures and flavours of baking, whether sweet or savoury, completely intoxicating.

In this book, I'm sharing some of my very favourite recipes that I hope will cater to your every baking need and whim. For those who aren't au fait with the oven, I've provided some simple basic recipes and techniques. If pastry's not your forte, for example, you'll find failsafe recipes for shortcrust, puff and choux on pages 234, 238 and 240. There are also recipes for other staples such as Classic Buttercream Icing on page 243 (the absolute best bowl to lick) and Crème Pâtissière (page 242). And, because I think it's often just assumed that everyone knows the basic baking techniques, I've provided comprehensive instructions for things like kneading dough by hand and toasting nuts (pages 244 and 245).

In every chapter, you'll find a whole host of tempting bakes: sweet and savoury, simple and more complex, traditional and unfamiliar. In Cakes, for example, I've included my foolproof Upside-down Summer Berry Cake

on page 37 (remember, baking isn't exclusively for those chillier months), and my go-to Rich Fruit Cake on page 57. These are the recipes I always rely on – they never let me down. You'll also find some slightly less well-known bakes, such as my Smørkage (page 42) – a divine treat hailing from Denmark – and my Chocolate Pain d'Épices (page 26), an intriguingly rich and spicy combination. Of course, a chapter on Cakes wouldn't be complete without a few show-stoppers. My particular favourite is the Brûlée Meringue Cake (page 18), which I love to flame to a lovely golden colour in front of my guests for some real cooking theatrics!

For me, biscuits are the easiest of bakes, and in this chapter I've provided a diverse range of recipes to suit all tastes. Everyone has their favourite, and for me it doesn't get better than a simple Chocolate Digestive Biscuit (page 78), and they taste all the better when they're freshly made. I'm also particularly fond of introducing different flavours to my batches – cinnamon and lemon, for example, or cranberry and orange, or even Parmesan and poppy seed (see pages 86, 84 and 92). It goes without saying that when it comes to cheese, there's no better accompaniment than a nice savoury biscuit, so I've provided my Crunchy Oatcakes with Sesame Seeds (page 95), and my Cheddar and Herb Biscuits (page 94), but be warned, they're incredibly moreish, especially with a chunk of Brie on top.

In the Sweet Bites chapter, you'll find a collection of tasty treats to satisfy those pesky sugar cravings. For me, cupcakes always hit the spot, so I've included a few of my favourites, such as lemon meringue (page 104) and Pear and Cardamom Buns (page 106). One of the best things about baking is the freedom it allows you to experiment and cater to your personal tastes. The Chocolate and Coconut Flapjacks (page 134), for example, encompass one of my all-time favourite flavour combinations – it will come as no surprise that I've always been partial to a Bounty bar! If your palate is piqued by something a bit more exotic, have a look at my Persian Almond Bites with Rosewater Syrup (page 136), which encapsulate some beautiful Middle Eastern flavours.

With all this talk of sweet treats it's easy to forget all the wondrous Savoury Bakes on offer. In this chapter, you'll find a recipe for every occasion. My Smoked Salmon, Tomato and Dill Tart on page 140, for example, is perfect for summertime picnics. In fact, I'm especially partial to a tart, and another favourite of mine is the Asparagus, tomato and spring onion version (page 151) – its gorgeously light yet luxurious flavour is perfectly

complemented by the crumbly shortcrust pastry. If you're having friends and family over for the evening and the white wine is flowing, the Cayenne and Sesame Cheese Swirls (page 166) and the Cheese and Rosemary Twists (page 170) are the perfect canapés. Thankfully, they're swift to make, so rustling up another batch when they've all been snaffled up isn't any trouble! In Savoury Bakes, you'll also find some hearty, warming meals for those brisk autumnal evenings, such as the Buttery Chicken and Mushroom Puff Pastry Parcels with Hollandaise Sauce (page 148), or my Smoked Haddock, Salmon and Prawn Pie on page 142. In truth, though, you really don't need an occasion or excuse to enjoy these savoury recipes – I've been known to knock up a batch of Pea and Cream Cheese Madeleines (page 160) on Sunday mornings for my family to enjoy throughout the day.

Leftover desserts, too, are often snacked on in my household. Desserts are a staple of any baker's repertoire, and in this chapter I've included lots of my favourites. There's a classic Tarte au Citron (page 190) with a subtle twist, a traditional rice pudding made with sweet saffron and condensed milk (page 195) and a Chocolate Pavlova with Salted Caramel Sauce (page 176), because who can resist such indulgence? You'll also find some more unusual bakes that make the perfect pudding, such as the Tarte Tropézienne on page 197. Originating from St Tropez, this elegant cake is made from a sweet, enriched brioche and is filled with creamy vanilla crème pâtissière – a real treat, and so luxurious.

Last but not least, you'll find plenty of mouth-watering dough-based recipes in the Breads chapter. I know many people with an aversion to baking loaves and scones and the like, but, honestly, they shouldn't be avoided – not least because they give off the best aromas in the process. I've provided recipes for the things you'd typically pick up in the supermarket, such as Croissants (page 214), Pain aux Raisins (page 216) and Naan Breads (page 222). Trust me, these are infinitely better and more satisfying when made from scratch. And you'll also find some slightly more off-piste recipes, such as my Jewelled Kanellängd on page 220: a wonderful plaited bread infused with the perfume of cardamom. Be sure to try the Southern Cornbread on page 218, too – it's delicious on its own (especially with extra Tabasco) and a great accompaniment to a warming chilli. It's also a good illustration of how diverse bread can be; from Chocolate Brioche Swirl Loaf (page 212) to scones (page 208) and doughnuts (pages 204 and 209), there's something in this chapter for everyone.

Whether you're a novice or a fully fledged baker, I hope that this book provides you with the resources and inspiration to explore all that the oven has to offer. These are truly some of my most loved recipes, and those of which my friends and family are particularly fond, too. So, whether it's a quick half hour snatched on a busy weekday evening to whip up some biscuits, or a long, lazy afternoon dedicated to crafting a beautiful celebration cake, find a window to enjoy the time-honoured and much-loved craft of baking.

Ingredients

Store-cupboard basics include flour (plain, self-raising and strong bread flour), butter, caster sugar, eggs and raising agents such as baking powder, bicarbonate of soda (bread soda) and yeast. Different flavours and interest are created by using combinations of whole or chopped nuts, ground almonds, seeds, dried or fresh fruit, spices, syrups, chocolate or the delicate flavours of vanilla, honey, lavender, rosewater or fresh herbs. If you like to bake often, you can keep a store of basics as above, but you could also buy whatever you need for recipes as you go.

Luscious finishes for cakes

For cake fillings and toppings, several recipes in the book have variations on the buttercream theme, with icing sugar and butter as their base. But you will also find fresh cream, cream cheese and crème fraîche toppings and chocolate glazes. I recommend buying plain chocolate with 55–62 per cent cocoa solids for use in the recipes in this book, as it has a rich flavour that works perfectly in bakes.

Baking with yeast

A range of recipes using yeast appear in the book, and it's worth understanding the types of yeasts available, as they are not all used in the same way. Fresh yeast can be bought from some bakers and, if properly wrapped up, lasts in the fridge for up to a month. Fresh yeast has to be activated by adding it to lukewarm milk or water and leaving it for 5 minutes or until it starts to become creamy. It is then added to the flour. You can also buy two kinds of dried yeast from supermarkets: active dried yeast is used in exactly the same way as fresh yeast, by first mixing it with liquid. Active dried yeast is twice as strong so you need to use half the amount compared to fresh yeast. Fresh fast-action, or easy-blend, dried yeast is mixed straight into the flour without pre-activating it. Most of the recipes in the book call for fresh yeast or active dried yeast.

Equipment

Your baking basics can be simply a large mixing bowl, a wooden spoon, a rolling pin, a baking sheet (with a lip on one side) and the most commonly used cake tins: a 20cm (8in) square cake tin and a 20cm (8in) round cake tin – preferably springform with high sides. With those few pieces you can make a variety of cakes and biscuits from this book, including small square cakes such as brownies.

Many biscuits are cut directly from a biscuit dough rolled into a sausage shape, but for others you will need a 6cm (2½in) cutter, either round or shaped. It is also essential to use accurate kitchen scales.

Oven temperatures are given for a standard oven; if you are using a fan oven, reduce the stated temperature by 20°C.

From muffins to smooth icings

You will need muffin and cupcake trays to make those popular small cakes, and both usually require paper cases to fit them.

Other sizes and types of tin appear in the book, including, most frequently: a 25 x 38cm (10 x 15in) Swiss roll tin for making flapjacks, cake squares, traybakes and focaccia; a 900g (2lb) loaf tin for making bread loaves and sweet tea loaves; two 20cm (8in) sandwich tins for making sponge sandwich cakes; and a loose-bottomed 23cm (9in) tart tin for baking savoury or sweet tarts.

A baking tray (with a lip all round) is used for toasting nuts. For melting chocolate you will need a heatproof bowl that can sit just inside

the top of a small saucepan. And a palette knife will enable you to create a smooth finish to a buttercream covering.

By hand or faster?

For speedy cake making, an electric beater will help you to cream sugar and butter together quickly – the basis of many cakes. A food processor will also do this for you. Most of the recipes in this book can be made without using a food processor or a stand mixer, although you can use them if you have them. A stand mixer, however, will make short and less tiring work of kneading yeast-based doughs.

Cakes

Brûlée meringue cake

Here is a creation from my friend and fellow Ballymaloe Cookery School teacher, Pamela Black, and it is such a fun cake to make. It starts so innocently, then ends with a mound of sugar and a flame! Do the brûléeing part in front of guests to delight them with some cooking theatrics.

Serves 8–10

225g (8oz) butter, plus extra
    for greasing
225g (8oz) caster sugar
1 tsp vanilla extract
4 eggs
225g (8oz) self-raising flour
225g (8oz) raspberry jam

For the buttercream icing

500g (1lb 2oz) icing sugar
225g (8oz) butter, softened
½ vanilla pod
2 tbsp milk
½ tsp vanilla extract

For the meringue

6 egg whites
350g (12oz) caster sugar

three 18cm (7in) sandwich
    tins; piping bag and no.
    7 plain piping nozzle;
    chef's blowtorch

1. Preheat the oven to 180°C (350°F) Gas mark 4. Grease the sides of the tins, and line the bases with baking parchment. Put the butter in a large bowl and cream it with a wooden spoon until soft, or use an electric beater on slow or a food processor.

2. Add the sugar and vanilla extract, and beat until light and fluffy. Beat in the eggs one at a time, adding 1 tablespoon flour each time and beating well after each addition. Sift in the remaining flour and fold in to combine.

3. Divide the mixture between the tins and bake for 20–25 minutes until well risen, golden and springy to the touch. Leave the cakes to cool in the tins on a wire rack for 2–3 minutes, and then turn them out on the rack to cool completely.

4. While the cakes are cooling, make the buttercream icing. Sift the icing sugar into a large bowl and add the butter. Beat until smooth using an electric beater or a wooden spoon. Split the vanilla pod lengthways and scrape out the seeds into the bowl. Add the milk and vanilla extract, and beat until the mixture is light and fluffy.

5. Put one cake on a plate and spread it with half the jam and a thin layer of buttercream. Put another cake on top and spread with the remaining jam and another layer of buttercream. Top with the remaining cake. Spread the remaining buttercream over the top and sides of the cake, smoothing the sides as you go. Leave in a cool place for at least 1 hour before you make the meringue.

6. Put the egg whites in a clean, grease-free bowl and whisk with an electric beater until they form soft peaks, or use a food processor. Whisk in the sugar until it forms very stiff peaks – this can take 15–20 minutes.

7. Fill the piping bag with the meringue mixture and, starting at the bottom of the cake, pipe 2.5cm (1in) blobs or discs on to the icing. Turn the cake clockwise by 2.5cm (1in) after each piping and repeat the process until the cake is completely covered with meringue.

8. Using a blowtorch according to the manufacturer's instructions, move it over the meringue in a circular movement until the surface of the meringue is a light golden colour. Serve.

Chocolate, honey and hazelnut cake

This incredible cake is gluten-free because it's made from ground hazelnuts instead of wheat flour. It's rich, nutty, chocolatey – and absolutely irresistible.

Serves 8

100g (3½oz) butter, plus
    extra for greasing
175g (6oz) dark chocolate
    (55–62% cocoa solids),
    roughly chopped
90g (3¼oz) honey
4 eggs, separated
100g (3½oz) hazelnuts,
    with skins
salt

For the chocolate honey glaze

100g (3½oz) dark chocolate
    (55–62% cocoa solids),
    roughly chopped
150g (5½oz) butter, cut into
    cubes
50g (1¾oz) honey

For the decoration

2 tbsp toasted hazelnuts
    (see tip, page 245),
    coarsely chopped
1 generous tsp honey

two 18cm (7in) sandwich
    tins

1. Preheat the oven to 180°C (350°F) Gas mark 4. Grease the sides of the tins, and line the bases with baking parchment. Put the chocolate and butter in a heatproof bowl over a saucepan of water, making sure the base of the bowl doesn't touch the water. Put over a medium heat and bring the water to the boil, then immediately remove the pan from the heat. Leave the mixture to melt slowly, stirring regularly.

2. Once melted (and the mixture is not hot), stir in the honey. Beat the egg yolks into the chocolate mixture.

3. Put the hazelnuts in a food processor and whizz until still a bit gritty. Add to the chocolate mixture. Put the egg whites into a clean, grease-free bowl, add a pinch of salt and whisk with an electric beater until they form stiff peaks, or use a food processor.

4. Fold the egg whites into the chocolate mixture in two halves, then divide between the two prepared tins and bake for 20 minutes or until a skewer inserted into the centre comes out clean. Leave to cool in the tins on a wire rack for 5 minutes. Run a knife around the edge and remove the cakes from the tins. Leave to cool on a wire rack, then remove the paper.

5. Meanwhile, make the glaze. Put the chocolate in a heatproof bowl over a saucepan of water, as before. Put over a medium heat and bring the water to the boil, then immediately remove the pan from the heat. Leave the chocolate to melt slowly, stirring regularly. Once melted, add the butter, a few pieces at a time, until it has all been mixed in and melted. Stir in the honey and place the bowl with the glaze in the fridge, stirring every 5–10 minutes and scraping down the sides of the bowl.

6. When the glaze has thickened, put one of the cakes upside down on a cake stand or plate. (You can use a plate turned upside down, which is quite convenient for icing the sides of the cake.)

7. Put some of the glaze on the top of the cake on the plate to cover it. Put the second cake on the first and then tip all the remaining glaze on top and, using a palette knife, spread it to cover the sides and top of the cake. To decorate the cake, scatter the toasted hazelnuts over the top and drizzle with the teaspoon of honey. Serve.

Triple chocolate celebration cake

Developed by my friend Pamela Black, this is a cake that doesn't need too much of an introduction – the title says it all! It's a guaranteed crowd-pleaser.

Serves 10 – 12

350g (12oz) butter, softened, plus extra for greasing
350g (12oz) caster sugar
6 eggs
350g (12oz) plain flour
2 tsp baking powder
40g (1½oz) cocoa powder
40g (1½oz) drinking chocolate
200g (7oz) natural yoghurt
110g (3¾oz) dark chocolate (55–62% cocoa solids), roughly chopped
gold leaf or icing sugar, to decorate

For the white chocolate buttercream filling

110g (3¾oz) white chocolate (melted and cooled)
225g (8oz) butter, softened
450g (1lb) icing sugar

For the chocolate glacé icing

110g (3¾oz) icing sugar
50g (1¾oz) cocoa powder
15g (½oz) butter
½ tsp vanilla extract

four 18cm (7in) sandwich tins; baking sheet

1. Preheat the oven to 180°C (350°F) Gas mark 4. Grease the base and sides of the tins, and dust lightly with flour. Put the butter in a large bowl and cream it with a wooden spoon until soft, or use an electric beater on slow or a food processor. Add the sugar and beat until light and fluffy.

2. Add the eggs, one at a time, adding 1 tablespoon flour each time and beating well after each addition. Sift the remaining flour, the baking powder, cocoa and drinking chocolate together in a bowl. Gradually fold into the egg mixture to combine. Finally, fold in the yoghurt.

3. Divide between the prepared tins. Bake for 20–25 minutes until firm to the touch. Leave to cool in the tins on a wire rack for 5 minutes, then turn out and leave on the rack to cool completely.

4. Meanwhile, make chocolate curls for the topping. Melt the chocolate in a heatproof bowl over a pan of gently simmering water, making sure the base of the bowl doesn't touch the water, and stirring regularly. Spread thinly over the back of a baking sheet and leave it to cool in the fridge until firm but not fridge-hard.

5. Hold a long, sharp knife at the top of the baking sheet and tilt it at an angle towards you with one hand on the handle and the other at the top of the blade. Very carefully pull the knife towards you, scraping the chocolate as you go. Curls should start to peel up from the sheet. If it crumbles, the chocolate is too cold, and if it goes gooey, it's too warm. Keep scraping down, returning the sheet to the fridge for a few minutes if it gets too warm, until you have shaved all the chocolate and collected enough curls for the top of the cake. Leave somewhere cool until needed. (They can be made a few days in advance.)

6. To make the buttercream filling, melt the chocolate in a heatproof bowl over a pan of gently simmering water, making sure the base of the bowl doesn't touch the water, and stirring regularly. Leave to cool.

7. Put the butter in a large bowl and cream it with a wooden spoon until light and fluffy, or use an electric beater on slow or a food processor. Sift in the icing sugar, beat well, then add 2 tablespoons hot water. Gently fold in the cooled melted white chocolate.

8. To make the icing, sift the icing sugar and cocoa powder into a bowl. Heat the butter, vanilla extract and 3 tablespoons water in a saucepan over a medium heat until just at boiling point. Pour into the icing sugar and cocoa, then beat well using a wooden spoon. The icing should be the consistency of fresh double cream; if it is too thick, add a little more warm water, then cool slightly before using.

9. Spread three cakes with half the white chocolate filling and then stack them together on an icing turntable. Put the remaining cake on top and carefully spread the top and sides with the remaining buttercream. Chill in the fridge for at least 1 hour until firm.

10. Gently pour the chocolate glacé icing over the top of the cake, allowing it to drizzle slightly and unevenly down the sides. Leave to set before piling the chocolate curls on top. Decorate with a little gold leaf for total decadence or dust the chocolate curls with icing sugar.

Chocolate pain d'épices

This cake is not overly sweet but it has an intriguing spice combination. It's worth splashing out on a really good high-cocoa chocolate bar that will add to the layers of wonderful flavours and aromas.

Serves 8

125g (4½oz) butter, plus extra for greasing
150g (5½oz) dark chocolate (55–62% cocoa solids), roughly chopped
150g (5½oz) caster sugar
3 eggs, lightly beaten
55g (2oz) ground almonds
¾ tsp ground cinnamon
½ tsp ground ginger
½ tsp ground cloves
½ tsp ground cardamom
icing sugar, for dusting
a mint sprig or an edible flower, to decorate
lightly whipped cream, to serve

20cm (8in) round springform cake tin with a high side

1. Preheat the oven to 160°C (315°F) Gas mark 2½. Grease the sides of the tin, and line the base with baking parchment.

2. Put the chocolate, butter and sugar in a large heatproof bowl over a saucepan of water, making sure the base of the bowl doesn't touch the water. Put over a medium heat and bring the water to the boil, then immediately remove the pan from the heat. Leave the chocolate to melt slowly, stirring regularly. When smooth, stir in the eggs. Fold in the ground almonds and then sift in the cinnamon, ginger, cloves and cardamom. Fold in to combine.

3. Pour the mixture into the prepared tin and bake for 40–50 minutes until the centre is just set. Leave to cool in the tin on a wire rack.

4. When the cake is completely cool, carefully take it out of the tin and put it on a serving plate or cake stand. Dust with icing sugar and decorate with a sprig of mint or edible flower. Serve with cream.

Glazed chocolate cake

Enjoy this unadulterated chocolate indulgence for the truest of chocaholics. I top this with beautiful crystallised rose petals to add some colour for an occasion, but if that's too much of a distraction from the chocolate, I understand.

Serves 8

125g (4½oz) butter, plus
    extra for greasing
150g (5½oz) dark chocolate
    (55–62% cocoa solids),
    chopped
150g (5½oz) caster sugar
3 eggs, lightly beaten
50g (1¾oz) ground almonds
crystallised rose petals
    (optional), to decorate
    (see page 192)

For the chocolate glaze

110g (3¾oz) dark chocolate
    (55–62% cocoa solids),
    chopped
2 tbsp milk
50g (1¾oz) butter

20cm (8in) cake tin

1. Preheat the oven to 160°C (315°F) Gas mark 2½. Grease the side of the tin, and line the base with baking parchment. Put the chocolate, butter and sugar in a large heatproof bowl over a pan of gently simmering water, making sure the base of the bowl doesn't touch the water. Melt the mixture and stir until smooth. Beat in the eggs, then fold in the almonds.

2. Pour the mixture into the prepared cake tin and bake for 40–50 minutes until the centre is just set. Leave to cool in the tin on a wire rack.

3. To make the chocolate glaze, put all the ingredients in a heatproof bowl over a pan of gently simmering water as before and melt together, stirring occasionally until smooth. Leave for 10 minutes to cool a little or until it has thickened slightly, but do not put the bowl in the fridge, as the mixture will lose its glossy sheen.

4. Transfer the cake onto a plate or cake stand, and pour the glaze over the top, allowing it to drizzle down the sides. I like to decorate this for a celebration with crystallised rose petals.

Dodo's Sachertorte

The mixture of dense chocolate cake, sweet apricot jam and that glossy, chocolate mirror glaze has made the Sachertorte a classic and much-loved dessert. This recipe is from Dodo, my fab brother-in-law. It takes a bit of time, but it's worth the effort.

Serves 10 – 12

150g (5½oz) butter, soft at
    room temperature, plus
    extra for greasing
½ vanilla pod
125g (4½oz) icing sugar
6 eggs, separated
125g (4½oz) dark chocolate,
    (55–62% cocoa solids),
    roughly chopped
100g (3½oz) caster sugar
150g (5½oz) plain flour,
    plus extra for dusting
200g (7oz) apricot jam
whipped cream, to serve

For the chocolate glaze

200g (7oz) caster sugar
200g (7oz) chocolate
    (55–62% cocoa solids),
    roughly chopped

24cm (9½in) springform
    cake tin

1. Preheat the oven to 170°C (325°F) Gas mark 3. Grease the side of the tin, and line the base with baking parchment. Scrape out the seeds from the vanilla pod and put in a large bowl. Add the butter and icing sugar, and cream with a wooden spoon until soft, or use an electric beater on slow. While continually mixing, add the egg yolks one by one to make a thick, creamy paste.

2. Melt the chocolate in a heatproof bowl over a pan of gently simmering water, making sure the base of the bowl doesn't touch the water, and stirring regularly. Leave to cool.

3. Use a spatula to scrape out the chocolate into the mixture in the bowl. Stir into the mixture using a wooden spoon, or with the mixer on slow. Set aside and wash the mixer blades for the next step.

4. Put the egg whites into a clean, grease-free bowl and add the caster sugar. Whisk with an electric beater until they form stiff peaks, or use a food processor. Put the egg white mixture into the first bowl and sift the flour over the top. Gently fold into the ingredients in the bowl using a wooden spoon until fully mixed together.

5. Pour the mixture into the prepared tin and gently even it out with the back of a wooden spoon. Bake for 45 minutes, turning the cake half a turn after 30 minutes. It's ready when a skewer inserted into the centre comes out clean.

6. Leave the cake to cool completely in the tin on a wire rack. Remove from the tin and remove the paper. Carefully transfer to a serving plate or cake stand.

Continued…

7. Gently dissolve the apricot jam in a small saucepan over a medium-low heat. Stir the jam and brush a thin layer all over the sides and top, then leave it to absorb into the cake.

8. Meanwhile, to make the chocolate glaze, put the sugar and 100ml (3¼fl oz) water in a small saucepan over a medium-high heat and bring to the boil. Boil for 5–7 minutes, then leave to cool.

9. Put the chocolate in a heatproof bowl over a saucepan of water and melt as before. Once melted, add the sugar syrup a little at a time, constantly stirring with a spatula or wooden spoon. It will try to thicken, so keep stirring and adding the syrup until it has a shiny, slightly thick, liquid appearance.

10. You need to work quickly at this stage, as the glaze needs to be poured over the cake while still warm. Starting at the edges and working inwards in a circular motion, and using the glaze in the bowl, brush it on to the sides of the cake and level any unevenness on the top with as few movements as possible. Allow the glaze to cool and harden. Serve with cream.

Ombré cake

Here is another of my friend Pam Black's creations. The ombré effect for icing is a simple idea but it makes an impressive-looking cake. If you are already nifty with a palette knife to ice cakes, this one is not too much of a stretch further. A turning icing table comes in handy, but alternatively you can use an upturned plate to put the cake on while you ice it. Pick whichever colours you like: go bright and pretty for a child's birthday, or keep to chocolates, caramels and vanillas for a more sophisticated look.

Serves 10 – 12

225g (8oz) butter, softened, plus extra for greasing
225g (8oz) caster sugar
4 eggs
1 tsp vanilla extract
225g (8oz) plain flour
1 tsp baking powder
2 tbsp milk, if needed

For the filling and topping

2 x quantity Classic Buttercream Icing (see page 243)
your choice of food colouring
your choice of fresh edible flowers or edible decorations

four 20cm (8in) sandwich tins

1. Preheat the oven to 180°C (350°F) Gas mark 4. Grease the sides of the tins, and dust lightly with flour, then line each base with baking parchment. Put the butter in a large bowl and cream it with a wooden spoon until soft, or use an electric beater on slow or a food processor. Add the sugar and beat it until light and fluffy.

2. Beat in the eggs and vanilla extract a little at a time, adding 1 tablespoon flour each time and beating well after each addition.

3. Sift in the remaining flour and the baking powder and fold in to combine, then add a little milk if needed to give a dropping consistency.

4. Spoon the batter into the prepared tins and spread evenly. Bake for 20–25 minutes until well risen, golden brown and springy to the touch. Leave the cakes to cool in the tins on a wire rack for 5 minutes, then turn them out on the rack to cool completely. Once cool, trim the tops off the cakes so that they are level.

5. Split the buttercream icing into four bowls. Use the food colouring to tint three of the bowls: one a pale colour, one medium and one a deep shade of the same colour.

6. Sandwich the cake layers on top of one another using the plain icing. Use a palette knife to cover the sides of the bottom third of the cake using the deepest colour icing. Cover the centre third with the medium icing, then spread the top third and the top of the cake with the pale icing.

7. Warm a clean, palette knife in boiling water, then run it around the cake sides to smooth out and blend the colours. Decorate the cake with flowers or as you prefer.

Mary Jo's tres leches cake

Mary Jo McMillin is the most wonderful cook and a great friend of everyone at Ballymaloe. She comes regularly from her home town of Chicago to spend time at the Cookery School and we all swap inspiration. This is Mary Jo's version of the famous three-milks cake: rich, yet not heavy, and completely delicious.

Serves 8 – 10

butter for greasing
150g (5½oz) plain flour, plus extra for dusting
5 eggs
1 tsp vanilla extract
150g (5½oz) caster sugar

For the filling and topping

225ml (8fl oz) fresh double cream
1 x 400ml (14fl oz) tin sweetened condensed milk
110–175ml (4–6fl oz) whole milk
1½ tsp vanilla extract
2 tbsp Grand Marnier or Cointreau (optional)
300ml (11fl oz) whipping cream
½ tbsp caster sugar
175g (6oz) raspberries

two 20cm (8in) cake tins; piping bag and medium star nozzle

1. Preheat the oven to 180°C (350°F) Gas mark 4. Grease the sides of the tins, and line the bases with baking parchment, then dust the sides with flour. Put the eggs, vanilla and sugar in a large bowl and whisk on high speed using an electric beater for 5 minutes until the mixture is pale and mousse-like.

2. Sift in the flour, then fold in thoroughly but lightly to retain the volume. Quickly divide the mixture between the two prepared tins and put in the centre of the oven to bake for 20–25 minutes until golden and a skewer inserted into the centre comes out clean. Cool the cakes in the tins on a wire rack for 2 minutes, then carefully turn out from the tins and remove the paper. Leave to cool completely.

3. To make the filling, put the cream in a large bowl and add the condensed milk, whole milk, 1 teaspoon of the vanilla extract and the Grand Marnier, if using. Mix together well.

4. Put the whipping cream in a bowl and whip until just holding its shape, then briefly stir in the sugar and remaining vanilla extract.

5. Using a small fruit knife, cut half the quantity of raspberries into halves. Put one layer of sponge on a serving plate, then use a cocktail stick to pierce holes over the surface.

6. Drizzle 200ml (7fl oz) of the condensed milk mixture over the sponge cake, then spread a thin layer of whipped cream on top and add the halved raspberries.

7. Top the berries with a thin layer of whipped cream. Put the second layer of sponge upside down on a plate. Make holes with a cocktail stick as before, then drizzle 3–4 tablespoons of the condensed milk mixture over the sponge. Now, quickly and carefully flip the second sponge layer over and put it on top of the first sponge. Poke more holes on the top of the sponge. Drizzle with a further 3 tablespoons of the condensed milk mixture until the cake feels moist but not very wet.

8. Spread the cake with some of the whipped cream, then pipe the remaining cream on top of the cake and around the sides and decorate with the whole raspberries. Chill in the fridge for at least 2 hours or overnight. Serve the cake with a drizzle of the remaining condensed milk mixture.

White chocolate and strawberry celebration cake

Here is a beautiful cake for a summer celebration. If made in the autumn, dark blackberries and blackberry jam would make a stunning substitute for the strawberries, providing a striking dark contrast against the white icing and chocolate.

Serves 10 – 12

250g (9oz) butter, plus
    extra for greasing
300g (11oz) caster sugar
3 large egg whites
1 tbsp vanilla extract
250g (9oz) plain flour
2 tsp baking powder
175ml (6fl oz) whole milk

For the topping

100g (3½oz) white
    chocolate, roughly
    chopped
250g (9oz) good-quality
    strawberry conserve
250g (9oz) strawberries,
    hulled
edible fresh flowers
    such as nasturtiums,
    roses, pansies, borage,
    marigolds, lavender or
    carnations (optional)
icing sugar, for dusting

three 20cm (8in) sandwich
    tins

1. Preheat the oven to 180°C (350°F) Gas mark 4. Grease the sides of the tins, and line the bases with baking parchment. Put the butter in a large bowl and cream it with a wooden spoon until soft, or use an electric beater on slow or a food processor. Add the sugar and beat until light and fluffy.

2. Whisk the egg whites and vanilla extract into the mixture well to add lightness. Sift half the flour and baking powder over the butter mixture and fold in. Add half the milk and fold again to combine. Repeat to add the remaining flour and milk, folding carefully so that you don't knock all the air out of the mixture.

3. Divide the mixture evenly between the prepared tins and bake for 20 minutes until they are risen and light golden, and a skewer inserted into the centre comes out clean. Remove the cakes from the tins and leave on a wire rack to cool completely.

4. Meanwhile, make chocolate curls for the topping. Melt the chocolate in a heatproof bowl over a pan of gently simmering water, making sure the base of the bowl doesn't touch the water, and stirring regularly. Spread thinly over the back of a baking sheet and leave it to cool in the fridge until firm but not fridge-hard.

Continued...

For the white chocolate buttercream

100g (3½oz) white chocolate, roughly chopped
2–3 egg whites, making 85g (3oz)
120g (4¼oz) icing sugar
240g (8¾oz) unsalted butter, softened and cubed

...Continued

5. Hold a long, sharp knife at the top of the baking sheet and tilt it at an angle towards you with one hand on the handle and the other at the top of the blade. Very carefully pull the knife towards you, scraping the chocolate as you go. Curls should start to peel up from the sheet. If it crumbles, the chocolate is too cold, and if it goes gooey, it's too warm. Keep scraping down, returning the sheet to the fridge for a few minutes if it gets too warm, until you have shaved all the chocolate and collected enough curls for the top of the cake. Leave somewhere cool until needed. (They can be made a few days in advance.)

6. To make the white chocolate buttercream, melt the chocolate as before, then leave to cool. Fill a pan one-third full with water and bring it to the boil. Put the egg whites in a grease-free, heatproof glass bowl and sift in the icing sugar. Take the pan from the heat and put the bowl over the pan. Whisk the egg mixture over the hot water using an electric beater until you have stiff peaks.

7. Remove the bowl from the pan and whisk until completely cold. At this point begin to add the butter, one piece at a time and whisking in before adding the next. This will take about 5 minutes. Once you have added all the butter, whisk in the melted and cooled white chocolate.

8. Put one of the sponges on a cake stand and spread over half the strawberry conserve. Carefully spread one-third of the buttercream over that, being careful not to mix it up with the jam. Put another sponge on top and repeat with the remaining jam and another one-third of the buttercream. Put the final sponge on top and spread over the remaining buttercream.

9. Arrange the strawberries around the outside of the cake, cutting larger ones in half, but leaving some whole. Pile the chocolate curls into the middle of the cake and add a few fresh flowers. Dust the cake with icing sugar and serve.

Upside-down summer berry cake

In the summer when berries are at their best, this is one of my favourite cakes to bake. There's something so fun about cooking the berries in a pan over the hob and then just pouring the batter over the top and popping the whole thing in the oven. Turned out, the mixture of berries makes the most beautiful ready-made topping, so there's no need to worry about icing – it's all ready to go. Team it with cream or ice cream and it makes a brilliant dessert warm from the oven, or allow it to cool and serve a slice with a cup of tea the next day.

Serves 8

50g (1¾oz) butter
200g (7oz) caster sugar
75g (2½oz) raspberries
75g (2½oz) blueberries
75g (2½oz) strawberries, hulled and cut into halves
200g (7oz) plain flour
1 tsp baking powder
½ tsp salt
¼ tsp bicarbonate of soda (bread soda)
2 eggs
1 tsp vanilla extract
200ml (7fl oz) buttermilk
75ml (2¼fl oz) sunflower oil
softly whipped cream, to serve

25cm (10in) ovenproof frying pan

1. Preheat the oven to 180°C (350°F) Gas mark 4. Melt the butter in the ovenproof pan over a medium heat. Stir in half the sugar and cook over a gentle heat for 2 minutes. Add the fruit and set aside.

2. Sift the flour, baking powder, salt and bicarbonate of soda into a large bowl. In a separate bowl, whisk the eggs. Add the vanilla extract, the remaining sugar, the buttermilk and oil to the eggs. Mix together to combine.

3. Pour the liquid mixture into the dry ingredients and whisk to form a batter. Pour the batter over the fruit in the pan. Put the pan in the oven and bake for 30–35 minutes until the cake feels firm in the centre.

4. Leave to cool in the pan on a wire rack for 5 minutes, then turn out by putting an inverted plate over the top of the pan and turning the pan and plate over in one quick movement. Serve warm or at room temperature with cream.

Lavender and lemon cake

Light as air, this Genoise-style cake is perfumed intensely with lemon and lavender. Those refreshing flavours are just what is needed to cut through the rich, fluffy meringue frosting on the top. If you don't have the sandwich tins specified, you can make the cake in a deep 18cm (7in) cake tin instead and slice it in half. Increase the cooking time to about 20 minutes – although the cake won't rise as much as it would when cooked in separate tins.

Serves 8 – 10

25g (1oz) butter, melted and cooled, plus extra for greasing
3 large eggs
90g (3¼oz) caster sugar
zest of 2 lemons
½ tsp culinary lavender, plus extra for sprinkling
75g (2½oz) plain flour

For the candied lemons

1 small lemon, thinly sliced
150g (5½oz) caster sugar

For the meringue buttercream

2 large egg whites
120g (4¼oz) icing sugar
240g (8¾oz) unsalted butter, cut into large dice and left to soften a little
½ tsp vanilla extract

two 18cm (7in) sandwich tins

1. Make the candied lemons in advance, as they will keep for a while. Boil a pan of water and drop in the lemon slices. Blanch for 1 minute, then lift them out carefully with tongs and leave them to drain.

2. Heat 150ml (5fl oz) water in a saucepan over a medium-high heat and add the sugar. Stir until the sugar has dissolved. Drop in the lemon slices and leave them to simmer gently for 20 minutes or until the skin is softened and sweet. Remove from the syrup using tongs and leave to dry on a piece of baking parchment.

3. Preheat the oven to 180°C (350°F) Gas mark 4. Grease the sides of the tins, and line the bases with baking parchment. Pour water into a saucepan to about 4cm (1½in) deep and bring it to the boil. Put the eggs and sugar in a large heatproof glass mixing bowl. Take the pan off the heat and put the mixing bowl over the pan, making sure the base of the bowl doesn't touch the water.

4. Using an electric beater, whisk the mixture until light and frothy. This will take 4–5 minutes, and when you lift the beaters out of the mixture, the batter dripping off the beaters should leave an impression for 3 seconds. At this point, take the bowl off the hot pan and continue whisking until the mixture is completely cold.

Continued...

5. Sprinkle in the lemon zest and lavender, then sift half the flour directly over the top of the mixture. Fold in, then add half the melted butter. Repeat to add the remaining flour, then butter, folding carefully so that you don't knock too much air out of the mixture.

6. Divide the batter evenly between the two prepared tins. Bake for 12–13 minutes until the cakes are shrinking away from the sides of the tins and are golden and firm to the touch on top. Remove from the oven and put a clean tea towel over the tins. After 5 minutes, turn them out on a wire rack and leave them to cool completely. If you aren't decorating them immediately, wrap them in cling film once they are cool – they will go stale quickly as they don't have much fat in them.

7. To make the meringue buttercream, prepare a saucepan of hot water as before. Put the egg whites in a clean grease-free glass bowl and sift in the icing sugar. Whisk over the hot water until you have stiff peaks. Remove from the pan and whisk until completely cold. At this point, begin to add the butter, one piece at a time, whisking in before adding the next. This will take about 5 minutes. Once you have added all the butter, whisk in the vanilla extract.

8. Spread about a quarter of the buttercream on top of one cake and put the other cake, base-side up, on top. Spread the remaining buttercream around the sides and on top of the cake. Lay the candied lemon slices on top and sprinkle with a little lavender.

Spiced pumpkin cake with cream cheese icing

Bake this wonderful cake when the weather turns chilly and pumpkins are at their best. Warmed with gentle spices, which are contrasted against a pure cream cheese topping, this is a comforting, autumnal delight.

Serves 8

275g (10oz) pumpkin
   (peeled and deseeded
   weight), grated
175g (6oz) plain flour
2 tsp baking powder
1 tsp ground ginger
1 tsp ground cinnamon
125g (4½oz) butter, melted
200g (7oz) soft light brown
   sugar
2 eggs
salt

For the cream cheese icing

250g (9oz) cream cheese
250g (9oz) icing sugar

900g (2lb) loaf tin

1. Preheat the oven to 180°C (350°F) Gas mark 4. Grease and line the base and sides of the loaf tin with baking parchment. Put a double layer of kitchen paper on a large plate. Check that you have the correct amount of grated pumpkin. Spread the pumpkin over the paper on the plate and leave to stand, to remove any excess moisture, while you prepare the remaining ingredients.

2. Sift the flour, baking powder, ginger, cinnamon and a pinch of salt into a bowl. Pour the butter into another bowl and add the sugar and eggs, then whisk to combine well. Add the grated pumpkin, then pour all of this wet mixture into the dry ingredients and stir to combine.

3. Pour into the prepared loaf tin and bake in the centre of the oven for 80–90 minutes until deep golden brown and cooked in the centre and a skewer inserted into the centre comes out clean.

4. Leave to cool in the tin on a wire rack for 10 minutes. Remove from the tin and leave on the wire rack to cool completely. Remove the paper.

5. Meanwhile, to make the icing, put the cream cheese in a bowl and sift in half the icing sugar. Mix to combine, then add the remaining icing sugar and mix again. Spread over the top of the cake. Cut into slices to serve.

Smørkage

This divine treat encompasses some of my very favourite ingredients: butter, almonds, cardamom and custard. Hailing from Denmark, there are many different versions of this cake, which are often enjoyed for brunch with hot coffee. Some of them are baked in a bundt tin and are then named butter ring. This is my version of the recipe and, although it does involve a few steps and a bit of time, I promise it is worth every single minute. What a treat this is – it might just be my favourite recipe in the book!

Serves 8 – 10

150ml (5fl oz) milk, lukewarm
50g (1¾oz) soft light brown sugar
25g (1oz) fresh yeast or 12g (½oz) active dried yeast
350g (12oz) strong white bread flour, plus extra for dusting
½ tsp salt
½ tsp ground cardamom
1 egg, beaten, plus 1 egg for the glaze
150g (5½oz) butter, cubed, plus extra for greasing
15g (½oz) almonds with skins

For the custard

250ml (9fl oz) milk
1 vanilla pod or 1 tsp vanilla extract
1 egg
50g (1¾oz) caster sugar
20g (¾oz) plain flour

1. Pour the milk into a bowl, stir in the sugar and crumble in the yeast. Leave to stand for 5 minutes until creamy. Sift the flour, salt and the cardamom into the bowl of a stand mixer with a dough hook. Add the beaten egg to the yeast mixture and pour on to the dry ingredients, then mix thoroughly until combined.

2. While mixing, add the butter, bit by bit until combined. It should be springy when you press the dough with your finger. The mixture will also come away from the sides of the bowl. It will take about 10 minutes.

3. Cover the bowl with cling film and leave to rise for 1 hour or until the dough has doubled in size. (Alternatively, put it into the fridge overnight.) The dough is ready when, having pressed it with a floured finger, the dent remains.

4. Meanwhile, make the custard. Pour the milk into a saucepan over a medium-high heat and add the vanilla pod (but not the vanilla extract). Bring to just boiling, then take the pan off the heat and leave the vanilla to infuse the milk for 5 minutes. Put the egg in a bowl, add the sugar and sift in the flour, then whisk for 1 minute until light.

5. Pour the milk on to the egg mixture, whisking all the time, then add the vanilla extract, if using. Make sure that the pan is clean with no trace of burned milk, pour the mixture back into the saucepan and whisk over a medium heat until boiling, then continue whisking for 2 minutes, in which time it will also thicken a lot. Pour into a clean bowl, then leave to cool.

...Continued

For the almond paste

100g (3½oz) butter,
   softened
150g (5½oz) soft light
   brown sugar
100g (3½oz) ground
   almonds
6–8 drops almond extract,
   to taste

For the icing

150g (5½oz) icing sugar,
   sifted
¼ tsp ground cardamom
1–2 tbsp boiling water

23cm (9in) springform cake
   tin; baking tray

6. Grease the side of the tin, and line the base with baking parchment. To make the almond paste, put the butter in a bowl and cream it with a wooden spoon until soft, or use an electric beater on slow or a food processor. Add the sugar, the ground almonds and the almond extract. Mix well, then set aside.

7. Once the dough is ready, tip it out of the bowl on to a floured work surface. Cut off one-third of the dough and cover the remaining dough with a clean tea towel. Roll the small piece of dough into a 25cm (10in) circle and put it into the base of the tin. Spread about 3 tablespoons of the almond paste over the dough to cover it, then top it with the custard, forming an even layer.

8. Roll out the remaining dough to a 28 x 40cm (11¼ x 16in) rectangle. Cover this with the remaining almond paste, then roll it up from the long side. Cut the roll evenly into 8 slices. Put one slice in the centre of the custard layer, cut-side up, then put the remaining swirls around the edge.

9. Cover the tin with cling film and leave to rise for 45 minutes or until light, puffy and doubled in size; when you gently press some dough with a floured finger the dent should remain. Preheat the oven to 180°C (350°F) Gas mark 4.

10. Beat the remaining egg with a pinch of salt and use to brush the cake, then bake for 30 minutes. Reduce the oven temperature to 160°C (315°F) Gas mark 2½ and bake for 20 minutes or until golden brown. Take the cake out of the oven and leave the oven on. Put the almonds on the baking tray and roast for 8–10 minutes until golden. Leave to cool.

11. Leave the cake in the tin on a wire rack to cool for 20 minutes, covered with a clean tea towel, then carefully run a small, sharp knife around the edges to free the cake from the tin, and unclip the sides. Turn it upside down to remove the tin base and the paper, then put it on a serving plate to finish cooling. Slice the cooled almonds coarsely.

12. To make the icing, sift the icing sugar and cardamom into a bowl. Add enough boiling water to make an icing the consistency of thick fresh double cream. Once the cake is cool, drizzle the icing backwards and forwards over the top of the cake in a zigzag pattern, then immediately scatter the toasted almonds over the top. Serve.

Coffee and cardamom cake

I absolutely adore cardamom, and there's something about its aromatic, smoky flavour that goes so well with coffee. I have paired them here in this luxurious cake, finished with a creamy mascarpone icing and toasted pistachio nuts.

Serves 8–10

175g (6oz) butter, softened,
    plus extra for greasing
175g (6oz) plain flour
175g (6oz) caster sugar
3 eggs, beaten
1 tsp ground cardamom
1 tsp baking powder
1 tbsp instant coffee
    powder
25g (1oz) pistachio nuts,
    toasted (see page 245)
    and chopped

For the coffee icing
250g (9oz) mascarpone
3 tbsp icing sugar
2 tsp instant coffee powder

two 18cm (7in) cake tins

1. Preheat the oven to 180°C (350°F) Gas mark 4. Grease the base and sides of the tins, and dust the sides lightly with flour, then line the bases with baking parchment. Put the butter in a large bowl and cream it with a wooden spoon until soft, or use an electric beater on slow or a food processor. Add the sugar and beat until the mixture is light and fluffy. Gradually add the eggs to the creamed mixture, beating constantly. Sift in the flour, cardamom, baking powder and coffee powder, and fold in gently to mix.

2. Divide the batter between the two prepared tins, making a slight hollow in the centres so that the cakes will rise with a flat top. Bake for 20 minutes or until well risen, golden brown and springy to the touch.

3. Remove from the tins and leave on a wire rack to cool completely. Meanwhile, to make the icing, put the mascarpone in a bowl and sift in the icing sugar and coffee powder, then mix well to combine.

4. Put one of the cakes upside down on a plate, then spread over half the icing. Put the other cake, right-side up, on top of the filling, then spread with the remaining icing. Scatter the toasted pistachio nuts over the top.

Gingerbread cake with raspberries

Based on a classic Victoria sponge, this beautiful cake has the added twist of warm spices. It makes a great layered cake for an occasion, piled high with sweet summer raspberries.

Serves 8

175g (6oz) butter, softened, plus extra for greasing
175g (6oz) plain flour, plus extra for dusting
175g (6oz) soft light brown sugar
3 eggs, lightly beaten
1 tsp baking powder
1 tsp ground cinnamon
1 tsp ground ginger
a pinch of ground cloves
¼ tsp ground cardamom
1 tbsp milk
125g (4½oz) raspberries

For the icing

125g (4½oz) butter, softened
125g (4½oz) cream cheese
275g (10oz) icing sugar
125g (4½oz) raspberries

two 18cm (7in) sandwich tins

1. Preheat the oven to 180°C (350°F) Gas mark 4. Grease the sides of the tins, and dust lightly with flour, then line the bases with baking parchment. Put the butter in a large bowl and cream it with a wooden spoon until soft, or use an electric beater on slow or a food processor. Add the sugar and beat until the mixture is light and fluffy.

2. Gradually add the eggs to the butter mixture, beating constantly. Sift in the flour with the baking powder, cinnamon, ginger, cloves and cardamom. Add the milk and fold in gently to mix.

3. Divide the mixture between the prepared tins and bake for 18–25 minutes, until golden on top and springy to the touch. Leave to cool in the tins on a wire rack for 10 minutes, then loosen around the edge of each cake using a small, sharp knife and carefully remove them from the tins. Leave the cakes on a wire rack to cool completely.

4. To make the icing, put the butter in a bowl or a food processor and add the cream cheese and icing sugar. Cream, or beat, until well combined and soft. Add the raspberries and gently mix together until incorporated.

5. Spread half the icing over the top of one cake and put the other cake on top. Spread the remaining icing on top of the cake. Decorate the iced cake with the raspberries, then serve.

Orange kugelhopf

I love my kugelhopf baking tin – it makes such grand, stately-looking cakes with very little effort! But, even if you don't have one, don't let that put you off trying this delicious orangey cake, because a 23cm (9in) springform cake tin will make a perfectly lovely cake, too. Drizzled with icing and sprinkled with pistachio nuts, it makes a great celebration cake.

Serves 10 – 12

225ml (8fl oz) sunflower oil, plus extra for greasing
325g (11½oz) plain flour, plus extra for dusting
1½ tsp baking powder
1½ tsp salt
400g (14oz) caster sugar
4 eggs
325ml (11½fl oz) milk
zest of 1 orange
25g (1oz) pistachio nuts, lightly toasted (see page 245) and chopped

For the icing

125ml (4½fl oz) crème fraîche
100g (3½oz) icing sugar, sifted
zest of 1 orange

23cm (9in) bundt tin or a 23cm (9in) cake tin with at least 4cm (1½in) sides

1. Preheat the oven to 180°C (350°F) Gas mark 4. Grease the bundt tin and dust with flour. (If using a cake tin, grease the side of the tin and line the base with baking parchment.) Sift the flour, baking powder and salt into a large bowl, add the sugar and mix together.

2. In a separate bowl, whisk together the eggs, milk and orange zest until combined. Tip this mixture into the dry ingredients and mix together using a wooden spoon to make a smooth batter. You may need to use a whisk briefly to remove any lumps of flour.

3. Tip into the prepared tin and bake for 50–60 minutes (or 60–70 minutes if using a cake tin) until the cake feels springy to the touch and a skewer inserted into the centre comes out clean.

4. Leave in the tin on a wire rack for 2 minutes, then run a knife around the edge of the tin and carefully remove the cake from the tin. Leave on the rack to cool completely, then remove the paper.

5. Meanwhile, make the icing. Put the crème fraîche in a bowl and sift in the icing sugar, then mix to combine. Add the orange zest and stir to combine.

6. Put the cake on a serving plate or cake stand. Drizzle the icing backwards and forwards from the centre to the outside of the cake in a zigzag pattern. Sprinkle over the pistachio nuts and serve.

Polenta, orange and pistachio cake with orange syrup

This gluten-free dessert is great for summer entertaining. Serve a slice on its own for a casual tea in the garden or add a good dollop of crème fraîche for a delicious dinner-party dessert. The syrup makes it so moist that you can prepare the cake in advance without the worry of it tasting stale.

Serves 8

225g (8oz) butter, softened,
  plus extra for greasing
125g (4½oz) polenta, plus
  ½ tbsp for dusting
225g (8oz) caster sugar
3 eggs
zest of 1 orange and juice of
  ½ orange
50g (1¾oz) pistachio nuts,
  roughly chopped
200g (7oz) ground almonds
1 tsp baking powder
25 pistachio nuts, lightly
  toasted (see page 245) and
  roughly chopped

For the orange syrup

75g (2½oz) caster sugar
juice of 1 orange

20cm (8in) springform cake
  tin with a high side

1. Preheat the oven to 170°C (325°F) Gas mark 3. Grease the side of the tin, and line the base with baking parchment. Dust the side of the tin with the ½ tablespoon polenta. Put the butter in a large bowl and cream it with a wooden spoon until soft, or use an electric beater on slow or a food processor.

2. Add the sugar and beat until light and fluffy. Beat in the eggs one at a time, then add the orange zest and juice. Add the pistachio nuts, ground almonds, polenta and baking powder, and fold in to combine.

3. Spoon the mixture into the prepared tin and bake for 55–70 minutes, until a skewer inserted into the centre comes out clean. If necessary, quickly put a piece of foil on top of the cake after 45 minutes of cooking, to prevent it from getting too brown.

4. To make the syrup, put the sugar and orange juice in a saucepan over a medium heat, and stir together until the sugar has dissolved. Once the sugar has dissolved, take the syrup off the heat and transfer to a heatproof jug.

5. While the cake is still warm, prick the top in a swirl pattern using a cocktail stick. Drizzle over the syrup.

6. Leave the cake to cool completely in the tin on a wire rack, then carefully lift it out and remove the paper. Put on to a serving plate or cake stand. Scatter the pistachio nuts on top and serve.

Walnut and fig cake with honey syrup

This cake has an old-fashioned feel, but its simple appearance belies its wonderful flavour: fruit, nuts, spice and honey combine in this delicious moist bake, which will mature and improve over a few days.

Serves 8

175g (6oz) butter, softened, plus extra for greasing
100g (3½oz) dried figs
175g (6oz) caster sugar
3 eggs
225g (8oz) plain flour
½ tsp ground cinnamon
1 tsp baking powder
2 tbsp milk
75g (2½oz) walnuts, roughly chopped

For the honey syrup

75g (2½oz) caster sugar
75g (2½oz) runny honey
1 tbsp lemon juice

20cm (8in) springform cake tin

1. Preheat the oven to 180°C (350°F) Gas mark 4. Grease the side of the tin, and line the base with baking parchment.

2. Put the figs in a saucepan. Add enough water to cover the figs. Bring to the boil over a medium-high heat, then reduce the heat and simmer for 2 minutes. The figs will be plump. Drain the water and put the figs on to a piece of kitchen paper to absorb any excess water. Set aside to cool. Remove the stems from the figs and cut each fig into 8 pieces.

3. Put the butter in a large bowl and cream it with a wooden spoon until soft, or use an electric beater on slow. Add the sugar and beat until light and fluffy. Add the eggs one by one, adding 1 tablespoon flour each time, and beating after each addition, then add the ground cinnamon.

4. Sift in the remaining flour and baking powder, then add the milk, walnuts and figs. Tip the mixture into the prepared tin, smooth the top and bake for 55–60 minutes until firm and a skewer inserted into the centre comes out clean.

5. Meanwhile, to make the syrup, put all the ingredients in a saucepan and add 100ml (3½fl oz) water. Stir together over a medium heat until the sugar has dissolved, then take off the heat and pour into a heatproof jug.

6. As soon as the cake comes out of the oven, prick it with a skewer in a swirl pattern and slowly drizzle the syrup all over the top. Leave to cool completely in the tin on a wire rack, then carefully lift it out and remove the paper. Put on a serving plate and cut into slices to serve.

Crunchy-topped apricot cake

Crunchy crumbles aren't just for chilly days – this one uses ripe, summer apricots, and you can keep the accompaniments light with fluffy whipped cream – although custard is still allowed if you must! Apricots have a real affinity with almonds, so I've added almonds to perk up the crumble mix.

Serves 8

100g (3½oz) butter, melted,
   plus extra for greasing
150g (5½oz) dried apricots
150g (5½oz) plain flour
1 tsp baking powder
½ tsp ground cinnamon
50g (1¾oz) caster sugar
1 egg
2 tbsp milk
lightly whipped cream,
   to serve

For the crumble topping

25g (1oz) plain flour
½ teaspoon ground
   cinnamon
25g (1oz) caster sugar
25g (1oz) butter, cubed
25g (1oz) almonds, with
   skin, roughly chopped
icing sugar, for dusting
   (optional)
whipped cream, to serve

20cm (8in) round
   springform cake tin

1. Preheat the oven to 180°C (350°F) Gas mark 4. Grease the side of the tin, and line the base with baking parchment. Put the apricots in a saucepan, then add 150ml (5fl oz) water or to cover them. Bring to the boil over a medium-high heat and then reduce the heat and simmer for 2 minutes. The apricots will now be plump. Drain the water from the apricots and put them on to a piece of kitchen paper to absorb any excess water. Set aside to cool, then cut each apricot into 4 pieces.

2. Sift the flour, baking powder and cinnamon into a large bowl, then add the sugar and stir well together. Make a well in the centre.

3. Put the egg in a bowl and add the milk and butter. Whisk together, then pour into the well in the dry ingredients and combine with a wooden spoon or a whisk. Beat well to make a smooth, thick batter, then spoon into the prepared tin and spread evenly. Scatter the apricots over the mixture and gently press them in with the back of a fork.

4. To make the topping, sift the flour and cinnamon into a bowl and add the sugar and butter. Rub the butter into the dry ingredients using your fingertips to make a crumb-like mixture, then add the almonds and stir well. Scatter the topping over the apricots.

5. Bake for 30–35 minutes until the top is lightly golden and a skewer inserted into the centre comes out clean. Leave in the tin on a wire rack for 10 minutes until cool enough to handle. Run a knife around the edge and remove the cake from the tin. Leave to cool on a wire rack, then remove the paper. Dust with icing sugar and serve with cream.

Rhubarb crumble cake

The vegetable that thinks it's a fruit – rhubarb – is one of my favourite ingredients to include in baked treats. The pretty, pink and deliciously tart rhubarb works perfectly under a crunchy, buttery crumble top.

Serves 8

125g (4½oz) butter,
   softened, plus extra for
   greasing
250g rhubarb, cut into 2cm
   (¾in) pieces
25g (1oz) caster sugar, plus
   125g (4½oz)
2 eggs
125g (4½oz) plain flour
1 tsp baking powder
icing sugar, for dusting

For the crumble topping

100g (3½oz) plain flour
50g (1¾oz) butter, cubed
50g (1¾oz) caster sugar

20cm (8in) round
   springform cake tin

1. Preheat the oven to 180°C (350°F) Gas mark 4. Grease the side of the tin, and line the base with baking parchment. To make the crumble topping, sift the flour into a bowl and rub in the butter using your fingertips until it resembles fine breadcrumbs. Stir in the sugar and set aside.

2. Put the rhubarb in a saucepan and add the 25g (1oz) sugar. Cook, covered, over a low heat for 6–8 minutes. Remove the lid and leave to cool.

3. To make the sponge base, put the butter in a large bowl and cream it with a wooden spoon until soft, or use an electric beater on slow or a food processor. Add the 125g (4½oz) sugar and beat until light and fluffy. Add the eggs one at a time, beating after each addition. Sift in the flour and baking powder, then fold together.

4. Spoon the batter into the prepared tin, then spoon the cooked rhubarb on top, and smooth the top using the back of the spoon. Sprinkle the crumble topping over the rhubarb and bake for 40–45 minutes until firm to the touch and lightly golden on top. Leave to cool completely in the tin on a wire rack, then carefully transfer to a serving plate. Dust with icing sugar and serve.

Coconut and orange cake

This is a lovely, not-too-sweet, cake that has a delicate flavour from the coconut and orange. It pairs well with the creamy, slight sourness of crème fraîche. I like to use a paper doily as a stencil for decorating this cake. It's quick and easy, and very pretty indeed.

Serves 8

100ml (3½fl oz) sunflower oil, plus extra for greasing
zest and juice of 1 orange
75g (2½oz) orange marmalade
2 eggs, lightly beaten
1 tsp vanilla extract
50g (1¾oz) caster sugar
50g (1¾oz) desiccated coconut
75g (2½oz) plain flour
1 tsp baking powder
salt
100g (3½oz) semolina
icing sugar (optional), to decorate

20cm (8in) round springform cake tin; doily (optional)

1. Preheat the oven to 180°C (350°F) Gas mark 4. Grease the side of the tin, and line the base with baking parchment. In a bowl mix together the oil, orange zest and juice, marmalade, the eggs and the vanilla extract.

2. In a separate bowl mix together the sugar and coconut. Sift in the flour, baking powder and a pinch of salt, then stir in the semolina.

3. Add the dry ingredients to the oil mixture and mix well until combined. It will be a wet batter at this stage. Spoon the batter into the prepared tin and bake for 25–30 minutes until a skewer inserted into the centre comes out clean.

4. Leave to cool completely in the tin on a wire rack, then transfer to a cake stand or serving plate. If you like, put a doily on top of the cake to use as a stencil and sift over icing sugar. Gently take the doily off and you are left with a pretty design.

Rich fruit cake

This recipe makes a large and deliciously moist cake. Because of all the fruit and alcohol, the cake keeps really well, and even if it does begin to move to past its best, a spreading of butter onto a slice will help to revive it. If you would prefer to keep it alcohol-free, simply omit the Grand Marnier or whiskey and add 50ml (1¾fl oz) extra tea instead.

Serves 8 – 10

250ml (9fl oz) warm strong tea
225g (8oz) soft brown sugar
50ml (1¾fl oz) Grand Marnier or whiskey
450g (1lb) dried fruit (sultanas, currants, raisins – sometimes I also add glacé cherries and candied peel)
butter, for greasing
2 eggs
zest of 1 orange
225g (8oz) plain flour
1½ tsp baking powder
2 tsp mixed spice
2 tbsp honey

23cm (9in) springform cake tin

1. Pour the tea into a large bowl. Add the sugar and stir in, then add the Grand Marnier or whiskey and dried fruit. Mix with a wooden spoon until combined. Cover with cling film and leave to stand overnight.

2. The next day, preheat the oven to 170°C (325°F) Gas mark 3. Grease and line the base and side of the tin with baking parchment. In a small bowl, beat the eggs and add to the fruit mixture. Add the orange zest, and sift in the flour, baking powder and mixed spice. Fold in to combine.

3. Pour the mixture into the prepared tin and bake for 45–55 minutes, or until a skewer inserted into the centre comes out clean. Brush with honey – it gives the cake a lovely flavour and looks great. Leave to cool in the tin on a wire rack, then remove the cake. Serve.

Clementine and almond cake

A wonderfully zesty clementine drizzle keeps this moreish almond cake moist and soft. It keeps well and is totally gluten-free. If you don't have clementines, you could use mandarins instead.

Serves 8

butter, for greasing
4 clementines
6 eggs
200g (7oz) ground almonds
200g (7oz) caster sugar
1 tsp baking powder
chopped pistachios and
    candied peel, to serve
crème fraîche, to serve

For the syrup

juice of 3 clementines
75g (2½oz) granulated sugar

20cm (8in) springform cake
    tin with a high side

1. Preheat the oven to 180°C (350°F) Gas mark 4. Grease the side of the tin, and line the base with baking parchment.

2. Put the clementines in a saucepan and cover with cold water. Bring to the boil, then reduce the heat and simmer, covered, for 2 hours, or until the clementines are cooked and soft. Drain the liquid from the clementines and set them aside to allow the fruit to cool.

3. Cut open each clementine and remove any pips. Finely chop each one, including the peel, making sure to include any juices from the fruit.

4. Put the eggs in a food processor and beat until light and fluffy (or mix in a bowl using an electric beater). Add the clementines, almonds, sugar and baking powder, and mix well.

5. Pour the mixture into the prepared tin and bake for 40–55 minutes until the cake is golden brown and a skewer inserted into the centre comes out clean.

6. Meanwhile, to make the syrup, put the clementine juice in a saucepan over a medium-low heat and add the sugar. Bring gently to the boil, stirring until the sugar has dissolved, then reduce the heat and simmer for 3 minutes.

7. While the cake is still warm, pierce it using a skewer and gently drizzle the hot syrup over. Leave in the tin on a wire rack to cool completely, then remove the cake from the tin. Remove the paper. Decorate with pistachios, candied peel and crème fraîche.

Banana and date loaf

Dates add a sweet, caramel flavour to this rich loaf cake – perfect for enjoying mid-afternoon with a cup of tea.

Serves 8 – 10

100g (3½oz) butter, softened, plus extra for greasing and to serve
250g (9oz) plain flour
1½ tsp baking powder
salt
150g (5½oz) caster sugar
2 eggs
1 tsp vanilla extract
4 small bananas, peeled
150g (5½oz) dates, pitted and chopped

900g (2lb) loaf tin

1. Preheat the oven to 170°C (325°F) Gas mark 3. Grease the side of the tin, and line the base with baking parchment. Sift the flour, baking powder and a pinch of salt into a large bowl. Add the sugar and butter, then rub in the butter using your fingertips until the mixture resembles coarse breadcrumbs.

2. Put the eggs and vanilla extract in a bowl and whisk. Add the bananas and mash well using a potato masher. Stir in the dates.

3. Make a well in the centre of the dry ingredients and pour in the banana mixture. Gently, but thoroughly, bring all the ingredients together using a wooden spoon, then pour the batter into the prepared loaf tin.

4. Smooth the top using the back of the spoon and bake for 1–1¼ hours or until a skewer inserted into the centre comes out clean. Leave to cool in the tin on a wire rack for 5 minutes, then remove from the tin and leave on the rack to cool completely. Serve sliced and buttered.

Ginger brack

Braic, or brack, is an Irish term for a fruited tea loaf, and this is my go-to recipe for a really good brack that gets even better after a couple of days. Once or twice, I have allowed the fruit to soak for two nights, because I have forgotten about it, and it does make an incredibly good, moist brack. If I want this in a hurry, and have not soaked the fruit overnight, I have boiled the tea, sugar and dried fruit for 2 minutes before adding the whiskey, then allowed it to cool completely before continuing with the recipe.

Serves 8 – 10

150g (5½oz) soft brown sugar
200ml (7fl oz) warm strong tea (it can be leftover tea)
50ml (2fl oz) whiskey
275g (10oz) dried fruit
1 egg, beaten
25g (1oz) stem ginger in syrup, drained and chopped
150g (5½oz) plain flour
1 tsp baking powder
2 tsp mixed spice
2 tbsp ginger syrup from the jar
butter (optional), to serve

900g (2lb) loaf tin

1. Stir the sugar into the tea, then add the whiskey and the dried fruit. Leave to stand overnight.

2. The next day, preheat the oven to 170°C (325°F) Gas mark 3. Line the loaf tin with baking parchment. Stir the egg into the fruit mixture, followed by the ginger, then sift in the flour, baking powder and mixed spice. Fold into the mixture well.

3. Pour the batter into the prepared tin and bake for 60–70 minutes until a skewer inserted into the centre comes out clean. Drizzle with the ginger syrup while the cake is still hot and leave to cool in the tin on a wire rack for at least 20 minutes before taking out. Serve in slices, with or without butter.

Biscuits

Coffee sandwich biscuits

If you like your coffee with a little more coffee on the side, these are a perfect solution! They aren't hard to make, but they look like you have made an impressive effort. You could even make them smaller and they would work perfectly as little petits fours to serve at the end of a meal.

Makes 12

100g (3½oz) butter,
   softened
100g (3½oz) caster sugar
1 egg, beaten
1 tbsp very strong coffee,
   cooled
175g (6oz) plain flour, plus
   extra for dusting
1 tsp baking powder

For the coffee butter icing

50g (1¾oz) butter, softened
100g (3½oz) icing sugar
1–2 tbsp very strong coffee,
   cooled

two baking sheets

1. Preheat the oven to 180°C (350°F) Gas mark 4. Line the baking sheets with baking parchment. Put the butter in a large bowl and cream it with a wooden spoon until soft, or use an electric beater on slow or a food processor. Add the sugar and beat until light and fluffy. Beat in the egg and the coffee.

2. Sift the flour and baking powder into the mixture, and stir to combine. Chill in the fridge for 30 minutes–1 hour. It will be a soft dough. With lightly floured hands, shape a heaped teaspoon of dough into a ball and put on the prepared baking sheet. Flatten slightly with the tip of your finger. Repeat to make 24 biscuits, spaced well apart. Bake for 9–11 minutes until just turning pale golden around the edges. Leave to cool on the baking sheet on a wire rack for 2–3 minutes, then transfer them to the rack to cool completely.

3. To make the icing, put the butter in a bowl and beat thoroughly with an electric beater, or use a food processor. Sift in the icing sugar and 1 tablespoon of the coffee. Mix well, then add a little more of the coffee to get a spreadable consistency.

4. Sandwich the biscuits together using a heaped teaspoon of icing. Put on a plate to serve.

Brandy snaps

One of the things I love about brandy snaps is that, depending on how you shape them, you can use them for so many different things: you can shape them into baskets and fill them with a rich chocolate mousse or ice cream; you can make chocolate-dipped cigarettes russes – perfect for sticking into ice cream; and the classic curved discs are great for adding crunch to creamy desserts such as possets or mousses.

Makes 10 – 12

50g (1¾oz) butter
50g (1¾oz) brown sugar
50g (1¾oz) golden syrup
50g (1¾oz) plain flour
¼ tsp ground ginger
¼ tsp ground cinnamon
2 tsp lemon juice
75g (2½oz) dark, milk
   or white chocolate
   (optional), roughly
   chopped

three baking sheets

1. Preheat the oven to 180°C (350°F) Gas mark 4. Line the baking sheets with baking parchment, making sure it is completely flat with no ridges. Put the butter in a small saucepan over a medium heat and add the sugar and golden syrup. Stir to melt the butter and dissolve the sugar, but don't allow the mixture to boil.

2. Take the pan off the heat and tip the mixture into a bowl, then leave it to stand for 2 minutes to cool slightly. Sift in the flour, ginger and cinnamon, stir to mix, then add the lemon juice, mixing well.

3. Put heaped teaspoonfuls of the mixture on the prepared baking sheets, spaced very well apart, as they'll spread out to about 12cm (4½in) in diameter. Spread the blobs out slightly using the back of the spoon. Bake for 8–10 minutes until deep golden brown and lacy in appearance.

4. Leave the cooked biscuits on the baking sheet for 1–2 minutes – if you try to remove them from the sheet too soon they will break, but if you wait until they are cool they will be too firm to mould into a shape.

5. If you want the brandy snaps to be flat, transfer them after 2 minutes using a fish slice or palette knife, to a cooling rack. If you want to mould them into shapes you need to remove them, carefully, from the tray while warm enough to be malleable but not so hot that they will collapse when trying to shape them.

6. To make baskets, put a small jam jar or bowl upside down on your work surface. Take the brandy snap off the tray, then flip it over to sit over the jar or bowl so that the lacy

side – the upper side in cooking – will be facing up when the bowl is made. Hold down the sides to mould into shape.

7. To make brandy snap rolls or cigarettes russes, roll the malleable brandy snaps around the handle of a wooden spoon with the lacy upper side facing out. Gently squeeze it tight to hold it in a roll for a few seconds to set. Transfer to a cooling rack to cool completely. Repeat with the remaining brandy snaps.

8. To decorate with chocolate, if using, melt the chocolate in a heatproof bowl over a pan of gently simmering water, making sure the base of the bowl doesn't touch the water, and stirring regularly. Dip the ends of the brandy snaps in the chocolate or drizzle the chocolate over them, then leave on a wire rack to cool and set.

Vanilla macarons

Here is the classic delicate French almond meringue biscuit (not to be confused with my Pine Nut Macaroons on page 111). The quantities might seem very precise, but they need to be to ensure a perfect result every time. Don't let that put you off – as with anything that is truly worth the effort, practice does make perfect!

Makes 20

60g (2¼oz) ground almonds
85g (3oz) icing sugar
65g (2¼oz) egg whites
　(2 medium egg whites,
　but weigh to be sure)
½ tsp vanilla extract
40g (1½oz) caster sugar

For the vanilla butter filling

75g (2½oz) butter, softened
1 tsp vanilla extract
40g (1½oz) icing sugar

baking sheet, piping bag
　and a 1cm (½in) plain
　nozzle

1. Preheat the oven to 160°C (315°F) Gas mark 2½. Line a baking sheet with baking parchment, making sure it is completely flat with no ridges. Put the almonds and the icing sugar in a food processor and whizz for 1–2 minutes until they are very fine. Tip out into a sieve over a mixing bowl.

2. Put the egg whites in a clean, grease-free bowl and whisk with an electric beater until they form soft peaks, or use a food processor, then whisk in the vanilla and gradually add the caster sugar while still whisking until it holds stiff peaks. To test for this stage, turn the machine off, lift the whisk out of the mixture and hold upright. The mixture on the whisk should be able to hold a stiff peak, rather than flopping over.

3. Tip half the almond mixture into the meringue mix and fold it in gently but thoroughly, using a metal spoon, then tip the remaining sugar and almond mix in and gently fold in to combine.

4. Put the mixture in the piping bag, then turn over and twist the top to close the bag. Pipe small rounds of the macaron mixture, as evenly sized as possible, about 3cm (1¼in) in diameter on the prepared baking sheet. They won't rise much, so they can be piped quite close to each other. You need 40 rounds. Give the tray a short, sharp tap on the work surface to ensure a good 'foot' on the macarons (the foot is the ruffle around the side of the macaron).

5. Bake for 15 minutes or until they are crisp on top and will lift off the paper without leaving any mixture behind. Leave to stand on the tray on a wire rack for 1 minute, then carefully slide them off the tray using a palette knife, and put on the rack to cool.

6. Meanwhile, to make the filling, put the butter in a large bowl and cream it with a wooden spoon until soft, or use an electric beater on slow or a food processor. Add the vanilla extract, then gradually add the icing sugar and beat in well until combined.

7. Using a small table knife, spread a generous layer of the filling on the flat side of a cooled macaron and sandwich with another. Repeat with the remaining macarons and filling, then serve.

Peanut kisses

Tasty and crisp, these cookies, formed into tiny bite-sized treats, make brilliant gifts. Pile them into gift bags tied with ribbon for friends, or just see how many you can balance around your teacup saucer!

Makes 24 – 28

125g (4½oz) butter, softened
75g (2½oz) caster sugar
50g (1¾oz) crunchy peanut
  butter
1 tsp vanilla extract
150g (5½oz) plain flour
2 tbsp roasted peanuts

two baking sheets

1. Preheat the oven to 180°C (350°F) Gas mark 4. Line the baking sheet with baking parchment. Put the butter in a large bowl and cream it with a wooden spoon until soft, or use an electric beater on slow or a food processor. Add the sugar and beat until light and fluffy.

2. Add the peanut butter and vanilla extract, and whisk again. Sift in the flour and mix until the mixture forms a dough.

3. Take a teaspoonful of dough and roll it into a ball using the palms of your hands. Put on the prepared baking sheet, spaced well apart. Using a fork, flatten each ball slightly, then put half a peanut, rounded side up, in the centre of each to decorate.

4. Bake for 10–12 minutes until lightly golden in colour. Leave to cool on the baking sheets on a wire rack for 2–3 minutes, then transfer them to the rack to cool completely.

Tuiles d'amande

These thin, crisp biscuits, which originate from Provence, are shaped to resemble the curved tiles that line the roof-tops of French country homes. They are lovely served with sorbets, ice creams and mousses, or just simply on their own. I enjoy the flavour and crunch that the flaked almonds deliver, but I'll sometimes experiment by scattering lavender, or even small dried rose petals, over the uncooked biscuits instead. These are also delicious using lemon zest instead of the orange.

Makes about 20

50g (1¾oz) butter
zest of 1 orange
2 egg whites
75g (2½oz) caster sugar
50g (1¾oz) plain flour
25g (1oz) flaked almonds

two baking sheets

1. Preheat the oven to 190°C (375°F) Gas mark 5. Line the baking sheet with baking parchment. Melt the butter with the orange zest in a saucepan over a medium-low heat, then set aside.

2. Put the egg whites in a clean, grease-free bowl and whisk with an electric beater until they form soft peaks, or use a food processor. Add the sugar and continue to whisk until smooth and glossy.

3. Add a quarter of the melted butter mixture to the egg whites, then sift in a quarter of the flour and gently stir in. Keep adding the butter and the flour in quarters in this way until it's all added.

4. Spread out teaspoonfuls of the mixture, spaced well apart, on the prepared baking sheets until just 2mm (⅟₁₆in) thick. Scatter over the almonds. Bake for 5–6 minutes until pale golden. Leave to cool on the baking sheet for about 10 seconds, then, while they are still flexible, lay them almond-side up over a rolling pin until cool and crisp. Tuiles will soften if they are kept in a moist, damp atmosphere, so as soon as they are cool, put them in an airtight container to store.

Cinnamon stars

I love giving these biscuits as Christmas gifts. They are so pretty, and I find that they work very well packaged in a clear bag, and tied with some festive ribbon. If you'd rather keep them for yourself, they do keep very well in an airtight container and can be made a few days before the Christmas rush!

Makes 25 – 30

2 egg whites
200g (7oz) icing sugar, plus
   extra for dusting
1 tbsp lemon juice
1 tsp ground cinnamon
225g (8oz) ground almonds
zest of 1 orange

two baking sheets; 6cm
   (2½in) star biscuit cutter

1. Line the baking sheets with baking parchment. Put the egg whites and icing sugar in a clean, grease-free bowl and whisk with an electric beater until they form stiff peaks, or use a food processor. Add the lemon juice and whisk until mixed together. Spoon one-third of this mixture (about 5 heaped tablespoons) into a small bowl and set aside.

2. Add the cinnamon to the remaining two-thirds of the mixture, followed by the ground almonds and orange zest, and fold in until well combined.

3. Lightly dust a work surface with icing sugar and turn out the dough. Gather into a ball and flatten slightly with your hands. Roll out the dough to 8mm (⅜in) thick and use the star cutter to cut out the shapes. Transfer to the prepared baking sheet.

4. Using a pastry brush, gently paint on the egg white mixture that you put aside earlier, to cover the star shape. Leave the baking sheets at room temperature, uncovered, overnight. They will dry out a little before you bake them the next day.

5. The following day, preheat the oven to 180°C (350°F) Gas mark 4 and bake the biscuits for 5 minutes. The white glaze on top of the biscuits will still be white and the biscuits will be moist inside.

6. Leave the biscuits to cool on the baking sheets on a wire rack for 2–3 minutes, then transfer to the rack to cool completely.

Iced lemon hearts

Sometimes the simplest things are the most well-received, and I find these unfussy iced hearts make a lovely token as a thank-you gift. They also cheer up a teatime table quite well – and they will keep for a week in an airtight container.

Makes 30 – 40

250g (9oz) plain flour, plus
   extra for dusting
½ tsp baking powder
100g (3½oz) ground
   almonds
100g (3½oz) caster sugar
125g (4½oz) butter, cubed
1 egg, beaten
zest of 1 small lemon and
   2 tbsp lemon juice
crystallised rose petals
   (optional), to decorate
   (see page 192)

For the icing

250g (9oz) icing sugar
2–3 tbsp lemon juice

two baking sheets; heart-
   shaped biscuit cutter

1. Line the baking sheets with baking parchment. Sift the flour and baking powder into a large bowl, then stir in the ground almonds and the sugar. Rub the butter into the dry ingredients using your fingertips until the mixture resembles fine breadcrumbs, or use a food processor.

2. Mix the egg with the lemon zest and juice. Pour into the dry ingredients and mix with your hands or a wooden spoon until you have a ball of dough.

3. Flatten the dough to about 1.5cm (⅝in) thick, then wrap it in cling film and chill in the fridge for 30 minutes (the dough can be kept in the fridge for up to 48 hours).

4. Preheat the oven to 160°C (315°F) Gas mark 2½. Roll out the dough on a lightly floured work surface to 5mm (¼in) thick, making sure to slide a palette knife or fish slice under the dough regularly to stop it sticking.

5. Using the biscuit cutter, cut the dough into heart shapes then transfer them to the prepared baking sheets. Bake for 12–16 minutes until the biscuits are golden and feel slightly firm around the edges. Lift off the baking sheets and carefully put on a wire rack to cool completely.

6. Meanwhile, make the icing. Sift the icing sugar into a bowl and stir in 1–2 tablespoons of the lemon juice. Gradually add a little more and keep stirring until you have a fairly stiff, but pliable, mixture.

7. Put a palette knife (or a table knife) in a jug of boiling water and use it to spread the icing over the hearts once they're almost cool. Leave to set in a single layer before storing them.

8. If you want to decorate the biscuits with crystallised rose petals, make sure that you put them on to the biscuits while the icing is still wet, then as it dries the petals will stick.

Chocolate shortbread hearts dipped in dark chocolate

These gorgeous little biscuits make a perfect edible gift, not just for Valentine's Day but for Mother's or Father's Day, anniversaries and engagements, too. I've used dark chocolate here for dipping, but there's no reason why you couldn't use white, milk or a mixture, if you prefer.

Makes 24

125g (4½oz) plain flour, plus extra for dusting
50g (1¾oz) cocoa powder
125g (4½oz) butter, softened
50g (1¾oz) caster sugar
100g (3½oz) dark chocolate (55–62% cocoa solids), roughly chopped

two baking sheets; 6cm (2½in) heart-shaped biscuit cutter

1. Line the baking sheets with baking parchment. Sift the flour and cocoa powder into a bowl. Put the butter in a large bowl and cream it with a wooden spoon until soft, or use an electric beater on slow or a food processor. Add the sugar and beat until light and fluffy.

2. Add the flour and cocoa to the butter and sugar, and mix until a dough forms. Turn the dough out on to a lightly floured work surface and flatten the ball of dough until it is about 2cm (¾in) thick. Wrap in cling film and chill in the fridge for 45–60 minutes until it has firmed up. Preheat the oven to 180°C (350°F) Gas mark 4.

3. Put the dough on a lightly floured work surface. Roll out to 5mm (¼in) thick and, using the biscuit cutter, cut out the dough and put it on to the prepared baking sheets. Bake for 10 minutes. Leave to cool on the baking sheets for 2–3 minutes, then transfer to a wire rack to cool completely. Line a baking sheet with baking parchment.

4. Melt the chocolate in a heatproof bowl over a pan of gently simmering water, making sure the base of the bowl doesn't touch the water, and stirring regularly.

5. When the shortbread is completely cool, hold each heart sideways and dip it into the melted chocolate to coat it halfway. Put the dipped shortbread on to the prepared baking sheet and leave in a cool place, but not the fridge, until completely cool and set.

Chocolate digestive biscuits

Yes, it's not hard to find a packet of digestive biscuits in even the smallest of local convenience shops, but they are not a patch on home-made biscuits fresh from the oven! You can go with milk chocolate, as here, or use dark or white, if you prefer; or if you omit the chocolate completely, these make a great biscuit to serve with blue cheese.

Makes 20–24

125g (4½oz) wholemeal
   flour
50g (1¾oz) porridge oats
¼ tsp bicarbonate of soda
   (bread soda)
½ tsp ground ginger
40g (1½oz) soft light brown
   sugar
75g (2½oz) butter, softened
1 tbsp milk
100g (3½oz) milk chocolate,
   roughly chopped

two baking sheets; 6cm
   (2½in) biscuit cutter

1. Preheat the oven to 180°C (350°F) Gas mark 4. Line the baking sheets with baking parchment. In the bowl of a food processor, mix together the flour and porridge oats. Continue mixing for 2–3 minutes until it resembles fine breadcrumbs.

2. Sift the bicarbonate of soda and ginger into the flour and oats. Add the sugar and mix until combined.

3. Whisk in the butter followed by the milk, and mix until a dough forms. Put the dough on a lightly floured work surface and roll out to about 5mm (¼in) thick. Using the cutter, cut out circles of the dough and put them on the prepared baking sheets. Bake for 10–12 minutes until lightly golden.

4. Leave to cool on the baking sheets for 2–3 minutes, then transfer to a wire rack to cool completely.

5. Melt the chocolate in a heatproof bowl over a pan of gently simmering water, making sure the base of the bowl doesn't touch the water, and stirring regularly. When the biscuits are completely cool, use a pastry brush to paint the melted chocolate over the top of each biscuit. Leave in a cool place on the wire rack until the chocolate is set.

lemon, polenta and rosemary biscuits

Gently scented with rosemary, these lovely golden biscuits are light and refreshing. The polenta gives them a tasty 'shortness' and an appealing snap. Try serving them with lemon tea.

Makes 35 – 40

100g (3½oz) butter, softened
75g (2½oz) caster sugar
zest of 1 lemon
2 egg yolks
150g (5½oz) plain flour, plus extra for dusting
75g (2½oz) polenta
2 tsp finely chopped fresh rosemary leaves
granulated sugar, for sprinkling

three baking sheets; 6cm (2½in) biscuit cutter

1. Line the baking sheets with baking parchment. Put the butter in a large bowl and cream it with a wooden spoon until soft, or use an electric beater on slow or a food processor. Add the caster sugar and lemon zest, and beat until light and fluffy.

2. Add the egg yolks, one at a time, adding 1 tablespoon flour each time, and beating well after each addition. Sift in the remaining flour and add the polenta and rosemary, then beat until combined.

3. Put the dough on a lightly floured work surface and knead for 1 minute to form a ball. Gently flatten to about 2.5cm (1in), then wrap it in cling film and chill in the fridge for 20–30 minutes until firm. Preheat the oven to 180°C (350°F) Gas mark 4.

4. Roll out the dough on a lightly floured work surface to 5mm (¼in) thick. Using the cutter, cut out circles from the dough and put on to the prepared baking sheets. Sprinkle a little granulated sugar over the top of each. Bake for 7–10 minutes until light golden in colour.

5. Leave to cool on the baking sheets on a wire rack for 2–3 minutes, then carefully transfer to the rack to cool completely. (The biscuits will keep for up to 1 week in an airtight container.)

Gingerbread trees

The fun starts long before you even tuck into these crisp, gingery biscuits. They are brilliant to make with children, who love rolling out the dough and stamping out shapes. I have gone with trees here, but you could vary the cutters to make them suitable for whatever occasion or time of year: hearts, snowflakes, a gingerbread family – whatever you fancy. You could also add colourful sweets, to decorate them, adding some 'fruit' to the trees!

Makes 45 – 50

350g (12oz) plain flour, plus extra for dusting
1 tsp bicarbonate of soda (bread soda)
1½ tsp ground ginger
1½ tsp ground cinnamon
125g (4½oz) butter, cubed
175g (6oz) caster sugar
1 egg, lightly beaten
100g (3½oz) golden syrup
icing sugar, for dusting (optional)

three baking sheets; tree-shaped biscuit cutter or other cutter

1. Line the baking sheet with baking parchment. Sift the flour, bicarbonate of soda, ginger and cinnamon into a large bowl. Rub the butter into the dry ingredients using your fingertips until the mixture resembles fine breadcrumbs, or mix together using a food processor. Stir in the caster sugar.

2. Add the egg and golden syrup to the mixture and beat until the mixture forms a dough. Put the dough on a lightly floured work surface and form it into a flat round. Wrap in cling film and chill in the fridge for 30 minutes to firm up. Preheat the oven to 180°C (350°F) Gas mark 4.

3. Roll out the dough on a lightly floured work surface to 5mm (¼in) thick. Using the cutter, cut out shapes from the dough. Put the shapes on to the prepared baking sheets and bake for 5–7 minutes until lightly golden brown.

4. Leave to cool on the baking sheet on a wire rack for 2–3 minutes, then carefully transfer to the rack to cool completely. Dust with icing sugar if desired.

Double ginger cookies

There were always ginger biscuits of some sort in a tin at my grandmother's house, and I can't eat ginger biscuits without thinking of her. These ones have been given an extra ginger hit with the addition of cubes of crystallised ginger for true ginger aficionados!

Makes 20

125g (4½oz) butter, softened
50g (1¾oz) soft light brown
  sugar
150g (5½oz) plain flour
½ tsp ground ginger
25g (1oz) ground rice
75g (2½oz) crystallised
  ginger, finely chopped

two baking sheets

1. Preheat the oven to 180°C (350°F) Gas mark 4. Line the baking sheets with baking parchment. Put the butter in a large bowl and cream it with a wooden spoon until soft, or use an electric beater on slow or a food processor. Add the sugar and beat until light and fluffy.

2. Sift the flour and ground ginger into the creamed mixture, followed by the ground rice and crystallised ginger. Beat to make a dough.

3. Divide the dough into 20 equal pieces and roll them into balls. Put them on the baking sheets spaced well apart. Wet a fork and use it to slightly flatten each ball, then bake for 12–14 minutes or until slightly golden in colour.

4. Leave to cool on the baking sheets for 2–3 minutes, then transfer them to a wire rack to cool completely.

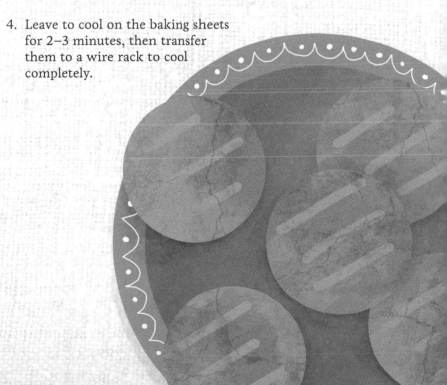

Vanilla and currant biscuits

Currants and a drop of good vanilla extract are a lovely way to add a little more interest to a simple light and crisp biscuit. These are popular with children and adults alike.

Makes 25 – 30

125g (4½oz) butter, softened
100g (3½oz) caster sugar
1 egg yolk, beaten
1 tsp vanilla extract
200g (7oz) plain flour, plus
    extra for dusting
½ tsp baking powder
salt
50g (1¾oz) currants
1–2 tbsp granulated sugar

two baking sheets; 6cm
    (2½in) biscuit cutter

1. Preheat the oven to 180°C (350°F) Gas mark 4. Line the baking sheets with baking parchment. Put the butter in a large bowl and cream it with a wooden spoon until soft, or use an electric beater on slow or a food processor. Add the sugar and beat until light and fluffy.

2. Add the egg yolk to the bowl followed by the vanilla extract, then sift in the flour, baking powder and a pinch of salt. Add the currants and mix until well combined to give a smooth dough.

3. Roll the dough out on a lightly floured work surface to a thickness of 5mm (¼in) and use the cutter to stamp out the biscuits. Arrange on the baking sheets spaced well apart, and chill in the fridge for 10 minutes. Sprinkle each biscuit with a little granulated sugar, then bake for 8–12 minutes until just turning pale golden. Leave to cool on the baking sheet for 2–3 minutes, then transfer to a wire rack to cool completely.

Cranberry and orange biscuits

I like to make these pretty golden biscuits, studded with cranberries, to give as gifts, especially at Christmastime. They store well in an airtight container for a few days, or you can freeze them. You could also freeze any of the leftover uncooked biscuit-dough log, then slice and bake it if you have a gift emergency!

Makes 20 – 30

125g (4½oz) butter, softened
75g (2½oz) caster sugar
zest of 1 orange
150g (5½oz) plain flour,
   plus extra for dusting
50g (1¾oz) dried
   cranberries

two baking sheets

1. Line the baking sheets with baking parchment. Put the butter in a large bowl and cream it with a wooden spoon until soft, or use an electric beater on slow or a food processor. Add the sugar and beat until light and fluffy.

2. Add the orange zest and mix until combined. Sift in the flour and add the cranberries, then mix until the mixture forms a dough.

3. Turn the dough out on to a lightly floured work surface and shape into a log about 25cm (10in) long. Wrap in cling film and chill in the fridge for 45 minutes to firm up. Preheat the oven to 180°C (350°F) Gas mark 4.

4. Using a sharp knife, cut the log into 8mm (⅜in) discs. Put each disc on the prepared baking sheets, spaced well apart. Bake for 8–10 minutes until slightly golden. Leave to cool on the baking sheets for 2–3 minutes, then transfer to a wire rack to cool completely.

Cardamom butter biscuits

These biscuits are packed with happy memories for me, as they remind me of the Danish biscuits we were given as children. They are light, crisp and buttery, and have a pleasing ring of crunchy demerara around the edge.

Makes 20 – 24

100g (3½oz) butter,
   softened
50g (1¾oz) caster sugar
100g (3½oz) plain flour,
   plus extra for dusting
50g (1¾oz) ground rice
½ tsp ground cardamom
2–3 tbsp demerara sugar

two baking sheets

1. Line the baking sheets with baking parchment. Put the butter in a large bowl and cream it with a wooden spoon until soft, or use an electric beater on slow or a food processor. Add the caster sugar and beat until light and fluffy.

2. Sift in the flour, ground rice and cardamom, and stir until a dough forms. Put the dough on a lightly floured work surface and shape into a log about 20cm (8in) long. Sprinkle the demerara sugar on to the work surface and roll the log into it, to ensure the surface is encrusted in sugar.

3. Wrap the log in cling film and chill in the fridge for 45 minutes to firm up. Preheat the oven to 180°C (350°F) Gas mark 4.

4. Using a sharp knife, cut the log into 5mm (¼in) slices. Transfer the slices to the prepared baking sheets, leaving space in between the biscuits. Bake for 8–10 minutes until slightly golden in colour. Leave to cool on the baking sheets on a wire rack for 2–3 minutes, then transfer to the rack to cool completely.

Cinnamon and lemon biscuits

Shortbread biscuits are a favourite with an afternoon cup of tea, and the cinnamon and lemon used here make them particularly refreshing.

Makes 20 – 25

125g (4½oz) butter, softened
125g (4½oz) caster sugar
zest of 1 lemon
200g (7oz) plain flour
1 tsp ground cinnamon
icing sugar, for dusting

two baking sheets

1. Preheat the oven to 180°C (350°F) Gas mark 4. Line the baking sheets with baking parchment. Put the butter in a large bowl and cream it with a wooden spoon until soft, or use an electric beater on slow or a food processor. Add the sugar and beat until light and fluffy.

2. Add the lemon zest and sift in the flour and cinnamon, then mix until combined. Take pieces of the dough and roll into walnut-sized balls using the palm of your hand. Put on to the baking sheets, spaced well apart. Using a fork, slightly flatten each one.

3. Bake for 10–14 minutes until pale golden. Leave to cool on the baking sheet for 2–3 minutes, then transfer them to a wire rack to cool completely. Dust with a little icing sugar and serve.

lemon and poppy seed biscuits

These tasty, speckled teatime treats are always well received. They use my trusty log technique, so you can slice a few discs off at a time, bake them when needed and freeze any leftovers. If the unthinkable should happen and you tire of the lemon and poppy seed combination, you can always make them with orange zest instead.

Makes 30

125g (4½oz) butter, softened
100g (3½oz) caster sugar
1 egg yolk
zest of 1 lemon
200g (7oz) plain flour, plus
    extra for dusting
½ tsp baking powder
1 tbsp poppy seeds

two baking sheets

1. Line the baking sheets with baking parchment. Put the butter in a large bowl and cream it with a wooden spoon until soft, or use an electric beater on slow or a food processor. Add the sugar and beat until light and fluffy. Beat in the egg yolk and lemon zest.

2. Sift the flour and baking powder together and add to the mixture, then add the poppy seeds and mix until combined to form a dough.

3. Turn the dough out on to a lightly floured work surface and shape into a log about 30cm (12in) long. Wrap in cling film and chill in the fridge for 40–45 minutes until firm. Preheat the oven to 180°C (350°F) Gas mark 4.

4. Unwrap the cling film and cut the log into 30 slices, 1cm (½in) thick. Put the slices on the baking sheet and bake for 8–9 minutes until just turning pale golden in colour. Leave on the baking sheets on a wire rack for 2–3 minutes, then transfer to the rack to cool completely.

Chocolate and hazelnut cookies

Part cookie, part cake, these delicious treats remind me of sipping coffee in an Italian piazza. The skins of the hazelnuts add a great flavour, as well as adding some health benefits (ahem).

Makes 20 – 25

100g (3½oz) butter,
    softened
100g (3½oz) caster sugar
1 egg, beaten
1 tsp vanilla extract
175g (6oz) plain flour
1 tsp baking powder
50g (1¾oz) hazelnuts,
    roughly chopped
50g (1¾oz) dark chocolate
    (55–62% cocoa solids),
    roughly chopped

two baking sheets

1. Preheat the oven to 180°C (350°F) Gas mark 4. Line the baking sheets with baking parchment. Put the butter in a large bowl and cream it with a wooden spoon until soft, or use an electric beater on slow. Add the sugar and beat until light and fluffy.

2. Add the egg and the vanilla extract to the butter and sugar mixture, and mix to combine.

3. Sift in the flour and baking powder, then add the hazelnuts and chocolate. Mix well. Roll pieces of the dough into walnut-sized balls using the palm of your hand. Put on the baking sheets, spaced well apart. Bake for 12–16 minutes until pale golden. Leave to cool on the baking sheets for 2–3 minutes, then transfer them to a wire rack to continue cooling. These cookies are delicious served slightly warm with a cup of coffee.

Oat and ginger cookies

The ginger taste in these cookies isn't an all-over flavour from using the ground spice. Instead, the toasted, nutty, oaty notes sing through, punctuated by sweet cubes of crystallised ginger, adding a little spicy kick to every bite.

Makes 25 – 30

200g (7oz) butter, softened
100g (3½oz) caster sugar
150g (5½oz) porridge oats
75g (2½oz) crystallised
   ginger, finely chopped
75g (2½oz) plain flour
¼ tsp bicarbonate soda
   (bread soda)

two baking sheets

1. Preheat the oven to 180°C (350°F) Gas mark 4. Line the baking sheets with baking parchment. Put the butter in a large bowl and cream it with a wooden spoon until soft, or use an electric beater on slow or a food processor. Add the sugar and beat until light and fluffy.

2. Add the porridge oats and ginger, and sift in the flour and bicarbonate of soda. Mix to form a dough. Take walnut-sized pieces of the dough and roll into balls using the palm of your hand.

3. Put on to the prepared baking sheets, spaced well apart, as they will spread a little. Bake for 10–14 minutes until pale golden. Leave to cool on the baking sheets on a wire rack for 2–3 minutes, then transfer them to the rack to cool completely.

Peanut butter and white chocolate cookies

The main dough ingredient in these flourless sweet, nutty cookies is the children's favourite – peanut butter – making them perfect for parties. Make sure you use crunchy peanut butter for a lovely knobbly texture. You can also easily vary the size of the cookies to suit the littleness of the children – little bites are very sweet for the under-fives!

Makes 25 – 30

200g (7oz) crunchy peanut
   butter
150g (5½oz) caster sugar
1 egg
1 tsp bicarbonate of soda
   (bread soda)
75g (2½oz) white chocolate,
   roughly chopped

two baking sheets

1. Preheat the oven to 180°C (350°F) Gas mark 4. Line the baking sheets with baking parchment. Whizz the peanut butter and caster sugar in a food processor, or using an electric beater, until pale and creamy.

2. In a separate bowl, whisk the egg and sift in the bicarbonate of soda (bread soda). Add to the peanut butter mixture and mix until combined. Stir in the chocolate.

3. Roll small pieces of the dough into walnut-sized balls and put on the prepared baking sheets, spaced well apart. Wet a fork, and slightly flatten each ball. Bake for 10–14 minutes until pale golden. Leave to cool on the baking sheets on a wire rack for 2–3 minutes, then transfer them to the rack to cool completely.

Parmesan and poppy seed biscuits

Both Parmesan and poppy seeds have such a strong flavour that these small biscuits really do pack a punch. They are brilliant as little bites on their own, as canapés or with cheese. You could also substitute the poppy seeds with sesame seeds for a completely different taste.

Makes 25

100g (3½oz) plain flour
100g (3½oz) butter, softened
100g (3½oz) Parmesan cheese, finely grated
1 tbsp poppy seeds

two baking sheets

1. Line the baking sheets with baking parchment. Put all the ingredients in the bowl of a food processor and mix until they form a soft dough. Alternatively, cream the butter in a bowl until very soft, then stir in the flour, Parmesan cheese and the poppy seeds.

2. Put the dough on a lightly floured work surface and shape into a log about 25cm (10in) long. Wrap in cling film and twist the ends so that it is airtight, then chill in the fridge for 50–60 minutes until firm. Preheat the oven to 150°C (300°F) Gas mark 2.

3. Unwrap the cling film, cut the log with a sharp knife into 1cm (½in) slices and put on them the prepared baking sheets spaced well apart. Bake for 15–18 minutes until just turning pale golden. Leave to cool for 2–3 minutes on the baking sheet on a wire rack, then transfer to the rack to cool completely.

Cheddar and herb biscuits

These biscuits are so simple to make, and so flexible. Use any herb that you have in the garden or buy a bag of your favourites. It takes seconds to make the dough in a food processor and you can freeze any of the dough that you don't use. They are great as a canapé, or just with cheese or olives for a quick snack.

Makes about 25

150g (5½oz) plain flour
125g (4½oz) butter, softened
125g (4½oz) Cheddar
   cheese, finely grated
1 tbsp finely chopped
   mixture of chives,
   rosemary and thyme
   leaves

two baking sheets; 6cm
   (2½in) biscuit cutter

1. Line the baking sheets with baking parchment. In the bowl of a food processor mix all the ingredients until they form a soft dough. Alternatively, put into a bowl and mix with a wooden spoon or an electric beater.

2. Turn the dough out on to a lightly floured work surface and shape into a log 25cm (10in) long. Wrap in cling film and twist the ends so that it is airtight, then chill it in the fridge for 50–60 minutes until firm. Preheat the oven to 150°C (300°F) Gas mark 2.

3. Unwrap the cling film, cut the log with a sharp knife into 1cm (½in) slices and put them on the prepared baking sheets. Bake for 15–18 minutes until just turning pale golden. Leave to cool for 2–3 minutes on the baking sheet on a wire rack, then transfer to the rack to cool completely.

Crunchy oatcakes with sesame seeds

These delicious crunchy oat biscuits, with their wonderfully nutty flavour from the sesame seeds, are just what I want to accompany a slice of cheese or charcuterie. The sea-salt flakes on top are, of course, optional, but they certainly enhance the oaty flavour even more.

Makes about 30

175g (6oz) rolled oats, plus
   1 handful
¼ tsp salt
¼ tsp baking powder
25g (1oz) butter, softened
25g (1oz) sesame seeds
1 tbsp olive oil
100ml (3½fl oz) boiling
   water, or as needed
sea salt flakes (optional), for
   sprinkling

two baking sheets; 6cm
   (2½in) biscuit cutter

1. Preheat the oven to 170°C (325°F) Gas mark 3. Put the handful of oats in a food processor and whizz until fine. Take out and set aside to use for rolling out the oatcakes.

2. Put the 175g (6oz) oats in the food processor, add the salt and baking powder, then whizz for 2 minutes or until the oats are finer in texture and look similar to ground almonds. Add the butter and the sesame seeds, and whizz until combined.

3. With the motor running, pour in the olive oil and then gradually add the boiling water, stopping frequently to check if the dough is coming together. Don't let it get too wet – you might not need all the boiling water, as it will depend on the oats. The dough should come together but not be too sticky.

4. Turn the dough out on to a work surface dusted with the fine oatmeal and knead just enough to bring it together. Roll out the dough to about 3mm (⅛in) thick, then sprinkle it with sea salt flakes, if using. Give the dough another light roll to make sure the salt stays attached.

5. Using the plain cutter or a knife, cut the dough into rounds, triangles or squares. Re-roll the dough scraps and cut out more. Put on the ungreased baking sheets and bake for 15–20 minutes until lightly browned on the edges and crisp. Transfer to a wire rack to cool completely.

Rye and caraway crackers

These Scandinavian-style crackers are perfect for piling with whichever toppings you fancy, whether that's smoked salmon gravadlax and dill or just your favourite cheese.

Makes about 36

150g (5½oz) wholemeal
   rye flour, plus extra for
   dusting
½ tsp salt
¼ tsp baking powder
1 tsp caraway seeds
15g (½oz) butter, cubed

For the topping

1 tsp caraway seeds
sea salt flakes, for sprinkling

two baking sheets; 6cm
   (2½in) biscuit cutter
   (optional)

1. Preheat the oven to 190°C (375°F) Gas mark 5. Sift the flour, salt and baking powder into a mixing bowl, then tip in any remaining bran from the sieve. Add the caraway seeds and mix well, then rub the butter into the dry ingredients using your fingertips to make a crumb-like mixture.

2. Make a well in the centre, pour in 75ml (3fl oz) water and mix to a dough – it should be a little soft and slightly sticky. Roll out the dough on a lightly floured work surface until 2mm (1⁄16in) thick, and dust the top of the dough with flour as well. Sprinkle the top with the caraway seeds and sea salt flakes, then lightly roll again to press the seeds and salt into the dough.

3. Cut into squares, or use the pastry cutter to cut into rounds, and put on the baking sheets (the crackers won't spread while cooking, so they don't have to be spaced far apart) and bake for 8–10 minutes until crisp and dry. Leave on the baking sheets on a wire rack to cool completely. (They can be stored for up to 3 weeks in an airtight tin.)

Sweet
Bites

Chocolate cupcakes with orange buttercream icing

You may notice from other recipes in this book that I have a particular fondness for chocolate and orange! These cupcakes are so pretty with their swirl of orange icing, scattered with green pistachio nuts. They are great for children's parties or treat days, but if you want to dial back the sugar a little, simply omit the icing and dust with a little icing sugar, and they are still delicious.

Makes 12

100g (3½oz) butter, softened
150g (5½oz) caster sugar
2 eggs, beaten
125ml (4½fl oz) milk
175g (6oz) plain flour
25g (1oz) cocoa powder
2 tsp baking powder
25g (1oz) pistachio nuts (optional), lightly toasted (see page 245) and roughly chopped, to decorate

For the orange buttercream icing

75g (2½oz) butter, softened
175g (6oz) icing sugar
zest of 1 orange and 1–2 tsp orange juice

12-hole muffin tray and muffin paper cases

1. Preheat the oven to 180°C (350°F) Gas mark 4. Line the muffin tray with paper cases. Put the butter in a large bowl and cream it with a wooden spoon until soft, or use an electric beater on slow or a food processor. Add the sugar and beat until light and fluffy.

2. Gradually add the eggs to the butter mixture, beating constantly. Pour in the milk and beat until well mixed. Sift in the flour, cocoa powder and baking powder, then mix gently to combine.

3. Divide the mixture evenly between the paper cases, filling each one two-thirds full. Bake for 20–25 minutes until well risen and lightly springy to the touch. Leave in the tray to cool for 5 minutes, then remove from the tray and put on a wire rack to cool completely.

4. Meanwhile, make the icing. Put the butter in a large bowl and cream it with a wooden spoon until soft, or use an electric beater on slow or a food processor. Gradually sift in the icing sugar and beat it into the butter, followed by the orange zest and enough orange juice to soften the icing to a spreadable consistency.

5. Spread a generous heaped teaspoon of the orange buttercream icing over the top of each cupcake in a swirl. If you like, decorate with a sprinkling of toasted pistachio nuts.

Banana and blueberry muffins

The banana in these fruity muffins keeps them soft and moist, and the blueberries practically qualify them as a breakfast food. Have one on the go at any time of the day – they are great for picnics, snacks and packed lunchboxes. If you prefer, swap the blueberries for raspberries or strawberries.

Makes 12

275g (10oz) plain flour, sifted
2 tsp baking powder, sifted
200g (7oz) caster sugar
4 eggs, lightly beaten
150ml (5fl oz) sunflower oil
1 banana, ripe and mashed
100g (3½oz) blueberries, fresh or frozen
salt

12-hole muffin tray and muffin paper cases

1. Preheat the oven to 180°C (350°F) Gas mark 4. Line the muffin tray with the paper cases. Sift the flour, baking powder and a pinch of salt into a large bowl and add the sugar, eggs and oil, then whisk together with an electric beater until smooth and well combined, or use a food processor.

2. Fold in the banana and blueberries. Divide the mixture evenly between the paper cases, filling each one three-quarters full. Bake for 20–25 minutes until well risen, golden and springy to the touch. Leave in the tray to cool for 5 minutes, then remove and put on a wire rack to cool completely.

lemon and poppy seed muffins

Poppy seeds and lemon go so well together and take these muffins a little bit beyond the ordinary. They are great for a lunchbox treat or a quick snack, and will keep well for a few days in an airtight container.

Makes 12

275g (10oz) plain flour
2 tsp baking powder
200g (7oz) caster sugar
2 tbsp poppy seeds
zest and juice of 1 lemon
4 eggs
150ml (5fl oz) sunflower oil
1 tsp vanilla extract

12-hole muffin tray and
    muffin paper cases

1. Preheat the oven to 180°C (350°F) Gas mark 4. Line the muffin tray with the paper cases. Sift the flour and baking powder into a large bowl. Add the sugar and poppy seeds, and mix together.

2. Put the lemon zest and juice in another large bowl and add the eggs, oil and vanilla extract. Mix well to combine, then add the dry ingredients to the lemon mixture. Mix together until well combined.

3. Divide the mixture evenly between the paper cases filling them three-quarters full and bake for 20–25 minutes until pale golden and springy to the touch. Leave to cool in the tray on a wire rack for 2–3 minutes, then transfer the muffins to the rack to cool – of course, they are delicious to eat warm too!

lemon meringue cupcakes

These wonderfully zesty cupcakes use meringue for a much lighter alternative to buttercream, while still having that characteristic swirl of topping. You can make your own lemon curd, or buy a jar of good-quality curd, and any left over can be enjoyed on hot buttered toast.

Makes 8

125g (4½oz) butter, softened
125g (4½oz) caster sugar
zest of 1 lemon
2 eggs, beaten
150g (5½oz) plain flour
¼ tsp baking powder

For the lemon curd

75g (2½oz) butter
150g (5½oz) caster sugar
zest and juice of 3 lemons
2 eggs and 1 egg yolk

For the meringue

2 egg whites
100g (3½oz) caster sugar

8-hole cupcake tray and
   cupcake paper cases

1. Preheat the oven to 180°C (350°F) Gas mark 4. Line the cupcake tray with paper cases. Put the butter in a large bowl and cream with a wooden spoon until soft, or use an electric beater on slow or a food processor. Add the sugar and lemon zest, and beat until light and fluffy. Gradually add the eggs, adding 1 tablespoon flour each time and beating well after each addition, then sift in the remaining flour and the baking powder, and mix to combine.

2. Divide the mixture evenly between the paper cases and bake for 7–10 minutes until risen and golden and the centre of each cupcake is slightly springy to the touch. Reduce the oven temperature to 150°C (300°F) Gas mark 2.

3. To make the lemon curd, put the butter in a saucepan over a low heat and add the sugar, lemon zest and juice, then heat very gently until the butter is melted.

4. Put the eggs and egg yolk in a bowl and beat thoroughly. Pour into the melted butter mixture and stir carefully over a low heat until the mixture has thickened and will coat the back of a wooden spoon. (If the heat is too high, the mixture will scramble. If it does, quickly remove the pan from the heat and push the mixture through a sieve into a bowl.) Remove the pan from the heat and pour the mixture into a bowl.

5. To make the meringue, put the egg whites into a large clean, grease-free bowl and whisk with an electric beater until they form soft peaks, or use a food processor. Gradually add the caster sugar while still whisking until the meringue holds stiff peaks.

6. Spread 1 teaspoon of lemon curd on top of each cake, followed by 1 tablespoon of meringue. Gently swirl the meringue to a soft peak. Bake for 9–11 minutes until the meringue is crisp on the outside, and marshmallowy and springy to the touch.

Pear and cardamom buns

Aromatic cardamom and subtle pear make a wonderful flavour combination in these unique cupcakes, and the fruit keeps the sponge soft and moist, too. If you aren't as big a fan of cardamom as I am, you can replace it with a few drops of almond essence or ½ teaspoon vanilla extract.

Makes 12

125g (4½oz) butter, softened
125g (4½oz) caster sugar
½ tsp ground cardamom
2 eggs
150g (5½oz) plain flour
¼ tsp baking powder
1 pear, peeled, cored and
    finely chopped
icing sugar, for dusting

12-hole fairy-cake tray and
    paper cases

1. Preheat the oven to 180°C (350°F) Gas mark 4. Line the fairy-cake tray with paper cases. Put the butter in a large bowl and cream it with a wooden spoon until soft, or use an electric beater on slow or a food processor. Add the sugar and cardamom, and beat until light and fluffy.

2. Add the eggs, one at a time, adding 1 tablespoon flour each time and beating well after each addition. Sift in the remaining flour and the baking powder, folding in to combine, then follow with the pear.

3. Divide the mixture evenly between the paper cases and bake for 10–12 minutes until golden and springy to the touch. Leave to cool in the tin on a wire rack for 2–3 minutes, then transfer to the rack to cool completely. Dust with icing sugar.

Blackberry and white chocolate buns

Sweet, soft and enticing, these buns are so popular with children, with their jammy baked berries and hidden chunks of white chocolate. Pop them into packed lunchboxes for a special treat or, served warm, they also make a great mini pudding. You could also try switching the blackberries for roughly chopped pecan nuts for a nutty version.

Makes 12

175g (6oz) icing sugar, plus
    extra for dusting
50g (1¾oz) plain flour
100g (3½oz) ground
    almonds
150g (5½oz) butter, melted
    and cooled
2 eggs, lightly beaten
50g (1¾oz) white chocolate,
    roughly chopped
100g (3½oz) blackberries,
    fresh or frozen

12-hole muffin tray and
    muffin paper cases

1. Preheat the oven to 180°C (350°F) Gas mark 4. Line the muffin tray with paper cases. Sift the icing sugar and flour into a large bowl. Add the almonds and stir to combine.

2. Pour the melted butter into the dry ingredients and add the eggs. Mix well, then fold in the chocolate. Spoon the mixture into the muffin cases and top each one with the blackberries.

3. Bake for 18–20 minutes until just firm in the centre. Leave to cool in the tin on a wire rack for 2–3 minutes, then transfer to the rack to cool completely.

Variation: For pecan and white chocolate buns, use 50g (1¾oz) pecan nuts, roughly chopped, as a topping instead of the blackberries.

Rose and pistachio choux kisses

As sweet canapés, these tiny choux bites look absolutely beautiful topped with bright green pistachio nuts and dried rose petals. And there's another lovely surprise awaiting guests when they bite into them and taste the delicate rose cream inside. Make sure you use a really good-quality rosewater for the best flavour.

Makes about 40

1 x quantity Choux Pastry (see page 240)
200ml (7fl oz) fresh double cream
½ x quantity Crème Pâtissière (see page 242), chilled
½ tbsp good-quality rosewater (I used Steenbergs)
200g (7oz) icing sugar
dried rose petals for sprinkling
50g (1¾oz) pistachio nuts, finely chopped

2 large baking sheets; piping bag with 1cm (½in) round nozzle and a small nozzle (about size 4); large baking tray

1. Preheat the oven to 200°C (400°F) Gas mark 6. Line the baking sheets with baking parchment. Spoon the choux pastry into the piping bag fitted with the 1cm (½in) nozzle.

2. Pipe small blobs of dough in rows on the baking sheets, leaving at least 1cm (½in) of space between them, as they will spread when baking. The dough will hold in the piping bag for a while, so it's easiest to pipe a trayful, bake them, and then pipe the other tray while the first is baking.

3. Bake the puffs for 15 minutes. Remove from the oven and, using a skewer, poke a hole in the bottom of each puff to release the steam. Return them to the oven for a further 5 minutes to dry out and finish browning.

4. Gently whip the cream until it is just starting to thicken. (If you whip it too firmly now, by the time you have stirred in the crème pâtissière it will be grainy and overwhipped.) Fold in the crème pâtissière and the rosewater, then transfer the mixture to a piping bag fitted with the small nozzle. Put the filled piping bag in the fridge to chill the mixture for 30 minutes.

5. Once the puffs are cool and the filling is chilled, pipe a small amount of the filling into the middle of each ball, using the hole you made with the skewer. Pack the balls on to the large baking tray so that they can't roll around.

6. Mix the icing sugar with enough water to make a fairly runny icing – you want it to be translucent and a brushable consistency rather than a thick mixture. Working on a few at a time, brush the tops of the balls with icing to glaze, then sprinkle with the rose petals and pistachio nuts. Leave to set before serving

Raspberry financiers

Financiers are not all they seem. Although they might look like simple little cakes, the key to their amazing, rich flavour is the beurre noisette, which gives the cakes a wonderful, nutty taste. The perfect financier should have a crisp golden exterior and a moist and rich almond sponge. Adding a raspberry doesn't hurt either.

Makes 12

100g (3½oz) butter, plus
    extra for greasing
90g (3¼oz) ground almonds
30g (1¼oz) plain flour
140g (4¾oz) icing sugar,
    plus extra for dusting
salt
3 egg whites
12 raspberries

12-hole financier tin or
    fairy-cake tray; baking
    sheet

1. Preheat the oven to 190°C (375°F) Gas mark 5. Grease the cake tin. Put the baking sheet in the oven to heat up. Fill the sink one-third full with cold water.

2. Put the butter in a saucepan and melt over a medium heat. Continue cooking for 5 minutes, swirling the pan occasionally so that the butter doesn't start to burn in places. The butter is ready when it starts to darken, smells rich and nutty, and you can see tiny specks of brown forming on the bottom of the pan. Take the pan from the heat and put it in the sink of cold water to stop the cooking immediately.

3. Put the ground almonds in a large mixing bowl and sift over the flour, icing sugar and a pinch of salt. Add the egg whites and mix gently, then, while still mixing, using an electric beater or a food processor, pour in the butter (the beurre noisette) in a steady stream and mix until well combined.

4. Divide the mixture evenly between the holes of the prepared tin and pop a raspberry in the centre of each one. Bake for 13 minutes or until risen a little and golden brown. Turn off the oven but leave the cakes to rest in the oven to finish cooking for another 5 minutes. Turn them out of the tin while still warm and leave to cool on a wire rack. Dust with icing sugar to serve.

Pine nut macaroons

My macaroons are a world away from the fluffy coconut macaroons, drizzled with chocolate, that we enjoyed as children – as delicious as they were. Pine nuts make these an altogether more intriguing and grown-up treat: nutty on the outside and moist on the inside, and perfect with after-dinner coffee.

Makes 12

100g (3½oz) ground almonds
75g (2½oz) caster sugar
1 egg white, lightly beaten
½ tsp vanilla extract
100g (3½oz) pine nuts

baking sheet

1. Preheat the oven to 180°C (350°F) Gas mark 4. Line the baking sheet with baking parchment. Put the almonds in a bowl and add the sugar, egg white and vanilla extract. Mix to combine into a slightly sticky dough.

2. Divide the dough into 12 pieces. Using dampened hands, shape pieces of dough into balls. Put the pine nuts on a plate and roll each ball in them so that they stick to the surface.

3. Put the encrusted balls on to the prepared baking sheet and flatten each one slightly using a damp fork. Bake for 12–15 minutes until lightly golden. Leave to cool on the baking sheet on a wire rack for 2–3 minutes, then transfer to the rack to cool completely. The macaroons can be stored in an airtight container for up to 3 days.

Cinnamon and pecan rugelach

Although these bite-sized treats might look fiddly, they are actually really simple and satisfying to roll up. They are quite sugary and do burn easily, so keep an eye on them when they are baking.

Makes 32

130g (4½oz) plain flour
salt
120g (4¼oz) cream cheese, very cold
120g (4¼oz) butter, diced and very cold
½ tsp vanilla extract
icing sugar, for dusting

For the filling

100g (3½oz) pecan nuts
50g (1¾oz) light brown sugar
50g (1¾oz) butter, softened
1 tbsp ground cinnamon
3 tbsp runny honey

two baking sheets

1. Line the baking sheets with baking parchment. Put the flour and a pinch of salt in a food processor and add the cream cheese, butter and vanilla extract. Whizz briefly for a soft dough. Alternatively, put into a bowl and mix well using an electric beater. Divide the dough into two pieces and put in plastic bags. Chill in the fridge for at least 2 hours.

2. Meanwhile, make the filling. Put the pecan nuts in the small bowl of a food processor and blitz to a coarse crumb, or chop very finely using a knife. Add the sugar, butter, cinnamon and honey to the processor and blend again to make a soft paste that's easy to spread. (Or mix well using an electric beater.)

3. Roll out a portion of pastry on a sheet of baking parchment dusted with icing sugar until you have a circle about 3mm (⅛in) thick. Spread half the filling over the whole circle. Use a large, sharp knife to cut the circle into 16 slim wedges.

4. Starting from the outside edge of one wedge, roll it up towards the middle. Move the pastry to the prepared baking sheet, tucking the tip underneath. Repeat with the remaining 15 wedges from the first portion of dough and then repeat with the second portion to make 32 pastries in all. Preheat the oven to 190°C (375°F) Gas mark 5. Put the baking sheets in the fridge to chill for 30 minutes.

5. Bake the pastries for 18 minutes or until golden brown – check them after 12 minutes or so and cover them with foil if they are already looking quite golden. Remove the trays from the oven and leave the pastries to cool on the sheet on a wire rack for 5 minutes before serving.

Raspberry and custard tartlets

Old-fashioned charm abounds in these wonderful custard tarts. Both the pastry and the crème pâtissière can be made in advance, and you can actually use any jar of jam that's been forgotten at the back of the cupboard – I just love raspberry. If you are going fancy with your tea party, pipe in the crème pâtissière using a star nozzle for a more elegant swirl.

Makes 18

1 x quantity Sweet
    Shortcrust Pastry (see
    page 235)
about 200g (7oz) raspberry
    jam
1 x quantity Crème
    Pâtissière (see page 242)
200g raspberries, to serve
icing sugar, for dusting

6cm (2½in) pastry cutter;
    two 9-hole mince-pie
    trays

1. Preheat the oven to 180°C (350°F) Gas mark 4.

2. Remove the pastry from the fridge and roll it out to 5mm (¼in) thickness, or a little thinner if you can. Using the pastry cutter, cut 18 rounds to line the mince-pie trays.

3. Spoon ½ teaspoon raspberry jam into each pastry case, then spoon 1 tablespoon crème pâtissière on top and smooth it to level.

4. Bake for 17–22 minutes until the pastry turns a light golden colour. Leave the tartlets to cool in the tin on a wire rack for 3 minutes, then carefully transfer them to the rack to cool completely. Decorate with the raspberries and dust with icing sugar before serving.

Mini carrot cakes with orange cream cheese icing

The flavours of carrot and orange go so well together, and using vegetables in baking can really help to keep your cakes moist. Ice them for a treat, but these can also be left un-iced and packed into lunchboxes. The iced cakes will keep for a few days in the fridge, or just in an airtight container without the cream cheese topping.

Makes 16

150ml (5fl oz) sunflower oil, plus extra for greasing
175g (6oz) plain flour
1 tsp baking powder
1 tsp mixed spice
150g (5½oz) caster sugar
3 eggs
1 tsp vanilla extract
225g (8oz) carrots, finely grated

For the orange cream icing

75g (2½oz) cream cheese, chilled
25g (1oz) butter, softened
zest of 1 orange
75g (2½oz) icing sugar

20cm (8in) square cake tin

1. Preheat the oven to 180°C (350°F) Gas mark 4. Grease the sides of the tin, and line the base with baking parchment. Sift the flour, baking powder and mixed spice into a large bowl.

2. Put the oil in another bowl and add the sugar, eggs, vanilla extract and carrot. Whisk together well. Add the dry ingredients to the carrot mixture and whisk until well combined. Spoon the mixture into the prepared tin and bake for 25–30 minutes until a skewer inserted into the centre comes out clean.

3. Leave to cool in the tin on a wire rack while you make the icing. Put the cream cheese and butter in a bowl and whisk until creamy using an electric beater, or use a food processor. Add the orange zest and sift in the icing sugar, then mix until the icing is smooth.

4. When the carrot sponge is completely cool, remove from the tin and put on a serving plate. Use a palette knife to spread the icing over the top. Cut into 16 squares and serve. The cake will keep in the fridge for up to 3 days.

Spiced ginger cakes

These sticky, treacly squares remind me of my dad, who loves gingerbread. There is something so comforting about a spiced, sweet, soft cake. These are so versatile, because they keep and travel well, so they are great for picnics or lunchboxes. Equally, they are good just kept in an airtight container at home, ready to have with a reviving mid-afternoon cup of tea.

Makes 16

75g (2½oz) butter, plus
    extra for greasing
75g (2½oz) soft dark brown
    sugar
100g (3½oz) black treacle
100g (3½oz) golden syrup
150ml (5fl oz) milk
1 egg, lightly beaten
225g (8oz) plain flour
1 tsp baking powder
2 tsp ground ginger
½ tsp ground cinnamon
¼ tsp bicarbonate of soda
    (bread soda)
½ tsp salt
50g (1¾oz) crystallised
    ginger, finely chopped
50g (1¾oz) sultanas

20cm (8in) square tin with
    high sides

1. Preheat the oven to 180°C (350°F) Gas mark 4. If the cake tin has a removable base, grease the sides of the tin and line the base with baking parchment, otherwise grease and line the base and sides of the tin with baking parchment. Put the butter, sugar, treacle and golden syrup in a saucepan over a medium heat.

2. Stir gently until melted and combined. Remove from the heat and whisk in the milk and egg. Put to one side.

3. Sift the flour, baking powder, ground ginger, cinnamon, bicarbonate of soda and salt into a large bowl. Make a well in the centre, then pour in the wet ingredients, the crystallised ginger and sultanas. Mix thoroughly, making sure there are no lumps of flour.

4. Tip the batter into the prepared tin and bake for 35–40 minutes until a skewer inserted into the centre comes out clean. Leave to cool in the tin on a wire rack for 10 minutes, then carefully remove the cake and leave it on the rack to cool completely. Transfer to a chopping board and cut into 16 squares.

Peach and almond squares

When peaches are at their juiciest and most fragrant, this is such a wonderful summery dessert. You could also make it successfully with nectarines, if that's what you have handy. The fruit will sink a little into the golden, almondy sponge, and soften on baking, making a mouth-watering combination. Serve with lightly whipped cream.

Makes 9

175g (6oz) butter, softened, plus extra for greasing
175g (6oz) caster sugar
3 eggs
175g (6oz) plain flour
1 tsp baking powder
100g (3½oz) ground almonds
5 peaches, cut in half and pitted
2–3 tbsp peach or apricot jam (optional)

20cm (8in) square cake tin with high sides

1. Preheat the oven to 180°C (350°F) Gas mark 4. Grease and line the base and sides of the tin with baking parchment. Put the butter in a large bowl and cream it with a wooden spoon until soft, or use an electric beater on slow or a food processor. Add the sugar and beat until light and fluffy.

2. Add the eggs, one at a time, adding 1 tablespoon flour each time and beating well after each addition. Sift in the remaining flour and the baking powder and add the ground almonds. Fold in to combine.

3. Spoon the mixture into the prepared tin and smooth the top using the back of the spoon. Put 9 halves of peaches in 3 rows of 3, cut side up (there will be half a peach over for the cook!).

4. Bake for 45–50 minutes until the sponge is pale golden and springy to the touch. Gently warm the jam in a small saucepan over a medium-low heat, and brush over the sponge and peaches while still warm. Serve warm or leave to cool.

Apple and lemon bites

Serve these moreish swirled squares warm for dessert, with custard or whipped cream, although they are equally good enjoyed cold the next day with a cup of tea. You can buy the apple sauce if time is short, or make your own – I have provided the recipe below.

Makes 9

175g (6oz) butter, softened,
   plus extra for greasing
175g (6oz) caster sugar
zest of 1 lemon
1 tsp vanilla extract
3 eggs
225g (8oz) plain flour
1 tsp baking powder
2 tbsp milk
250ml (9fl oz) apple sauce
   (bought or home-made,
   see tip)
icing sugar, for dusting
custard or whipped cream,
   to serve

20cm (8in) square cake tin
   with high sides

1. Preheat the oven to 180°C (350°F) Gas mark 4. Grease and line the base and sides of the tin with baking parchment. Put the butter in a large bowl and cream it with a wooden spoon until soft, or use an electric beater on slow or a food processor. Add the sugar and beat until light and fluffy.

2. Add the lemon zest and vanilla extract, and mix to combine. Add the eggs, one at a time, adding 1 tablespoon flour each time and beating well after each addition. Sift in the remaining flour and the baking powder and fold in, followed by the milk.

3. Spoon half the batter into the prepared tin, then spoon the apple sauce to cover the surface of the cake mixture. Cover the apple sauce with the remaining half of the cake batter. Using a skewer, gently swirl in a figure-of-eight motion, without touching the base of the tin, to gently distribute the apple sauce into the cake mixture.

4. Bake for 35–45 minutes until a skewer inserted into the centre comes out clean. Leave to cool in the tin for 2–3 minutes, then cut into 9 squares, dust with icing sugar and enjoy warm with custard or cream.

Tip: To make apple sauce, peel, quarter and core 350g (12oz) cooking apples. Cut the quarters in half and put in a heavy-based saucepan with 50g (1¾oz) caster or granulated sugar and 1–2 tablespoons water. Cover and heat gently. As soon as the apples have broken down, remove the pan from the heat and beat into a purée using a wooden spoon. Stir and taste for sweetness, adding more sugar if needed.

Date, coconut and orange squares

These nutty, fruity squares are great for popping into picnics and lunchboxes. The sticky dates keep them from drying out, so they will keep for up to a week in an airtight box, and they also freeze well.

Makes 16

200g (7oz) pitted dates, chopped
175g (6oz) plain flour
½ tsp bicarbonate of soda (bread soda)
175g (6oz) caster sugar
75g (2½oz) porridge oats
25g (1oz) desiccated coconut
zest of 1 orange
salt
175g (6oz) butter, cubed

20cm (8in) square cake tin

1. Preheat the oven to 180°C (350°F) Gas mark 4. Grease the sides of the tin, and line the base with baking parchment. Put the dates in a saucepan and add 250ml (9fl oz) water. Bring to a simmer over a medium heat, then reduce the heat to medium-low and cook for 10 minutes or until the date mixture is very soft and thick, stirring occasionally. Remove from the heat and leave to cool to room temperature.

2. Sift the flour and bicarbonate of soda into a large bowl. Add the sugar, oats, coconut, orange zest and a pinch of salt. Mix well. Add the butter and, using your fingertips, rub it in until moist clumps form.

3. Press half the oat mixture evenly over the base of the prepared tin. Spread the cooked date mixture over this, then sprinkle with the remaining oat mixture. Press gently with the palm of your hand to flatten it on top.

4. Bake for 40 minutes or until golden brown at the edges and set in the centre. Leave to cool completely in the tin on a wire rack, then cut into squares and serve.

Lime-glazed coconut cakes

Delight your visiting friends with this soft sponge and its wonderful tangy lime glaze. Lime and coconut make a wonderful pairing: it can bring a touch of the tropical to your afternoon tea – which can be especially welcome on a grey day!

Makes 18 – 24

175g (6oz) butter, softened, plus extra for greasing
zest of 2 limes
175g (6oz) caster sugar
3 eggs
225g (8oz) plain flour
1 tsp baking powder
75g (2½oz) desiccated coconut
2 tbsp milk

For the lime glaze

juice of 2 limes
100g (3½oz) caster sugar

33 x 23cm (13 x 9in) Swiss roll tin

1. Preheat the oven to 180°C (350°F) Gas mark 4. Grease the base and sides of the tin. Put the butter and lime zest in a large bowl and cream with a wooden spoon until soft, or use an electric beater on slow or a food processor. Add the caster sugar and beat until pale and creamy.

2. Beat in the eggs, one at a time, then sift in the flour and baking powder, and add the desiccated coconut. Fold in well, then stir in the milk.

3. Spoon the batter into the prepared tin and bake for 15–20 minutes until a skewer inserted into the centre comes out clean.

4. Meanwhile, to make the glaze, mix the lime juice and sugar together in a jug or small bowl. As soon as the sponge comes out of the oven, prick all over the surface with a skewer or cocktail stick. Gently pour or spoon the glaze over the top of the sponge, allowing the glaze to sink in. Cool completely before transferring to a chopping board and cutting into 18 or 24 squares and serving.

Raspberry crumbles

My family can't get enough of these crumble squares – that combination of sweet roasted fruit and golden, crisp crumble is just timeless. You can use blueberries instead of raspberries, if you prefer, or even half and half.

Makes 16

175g (6oz) butter, softened,
  plus extra for greasing
175g (6oz) caster sugar
2 eggs, beaten
50ml (1¾fl oz) milk
100g (3½oz) plain flour
75g (2½oz) wholemeal flour
1 tsp baking powder
½ tsp ground cinnamon
150g (5½oz) fresh or frozen
  raspberries
icing sugar, for dusting
whipped cream, to serve

For the crumble topping

100g (3½oz) plain flour
50g (1¾oz) butter, cubed
50g (1¾oz) soft light brown
  sugar
½ tsp ground cinnamon

20cm (8in) square cake tin
  with high sides

1. Preheat the oven to 180°C (350°F) Gas mark 4. Grease and line the base and sides of the tin with baking parchment. Put the butter in a large bowl and cream it with a wooden spoon until soft, or use an electric beater on slow or a food processor. Add the sugar and beat until the mixture is light and fluffy.

2. Add the eggs to the mixture followed by the milk, beating constantly until well combined.

3. Sift in the flours, baking powder and ground cinnamon, adding any bran left in the sieve, then fold in to combine. Fold in the raspberries. Spoon the mixture into the prepared tin.

4. To make the crumble topping, sift the flour into a bowl and rub in the butter using your fingertips until it resembles fine breadcrumbs, or use a food processor. Stir in the sugar and the cinnamon. Spoon the crumble mixture over the sponge mixture in the tin, making sure that you cover the sponge all over.

5. Bake for 40–50 minutes until a skewer inserted into the centre comes out clean. Leave to cool in the tin on a wire rack for 5–10 minutes, then cut into squares. Cool, then gently remove the squares from the tin and serve them with a dusting of icing sugar and some whipped cream.

Strawberry and raspberry squares

Here is the perfect excuse for a trip to the local pick-your-own farm! Strawberries and raspberries sing of summer, but you can tumble in blueberries, blackberries and even red- or white currants for a touch of sharpness. This traybake is so simple to make and informal; it's perfect with tea in the garden or as a dessert with cream or custard. If you don't have a lemon to hand, try using orange zest instead.

Makes 16

175g (6oz) butter, softened,
   plus extra for greasing
175g (6oz) caster sugar
2 eggs, lightly beaten
zest of 1 orange
50ml (1¾fl oz) milk
175g (6oz) plain flour
1 tsp baking powder
100g (3½oz) raspberries
100g (3½oz) strawberries,
   hulled and cut into
   quarters
icing sugar, for dusting

20cm (8in) square cake tin
   with high sides

1. Preheat the oven to 180°C (350°F) Gas mark 4. If the cake tin has a removable base, grease the sides of the tin and line the base with baking parchment, otherwise grease and line the base and sides of the tin. Put the butter in a large bowl and cream it with a wooden spoon until soft, or use an electric beater on slow or a food processor.

2. Add the caster sugar and beat until light and fluffy. Gradually add the eggs to the butter mixture, beating constantly. Beat in the orange zest and the milk.

3. Sift in the flour and baking powder, then fold in to combine. Add 50g (1¾oz) of the raspberries and 50g (1¾oz) of the strawberries, and gently fold in. Tip the mixture into the prepared tin, then dot the remaining raspberries and strawberries over the top of the cake mixture. Bake for 30–35 minutes until a skewer inserted into the centre comes out clean.

4. Leave to cool in the tin on a wire rack for 10 minutes, then carefully remove the cake and leave on the wire rack to cool completely before transferring to a chopping board and cutting into 16 squares.

Chocolate orange brownies

The perfect pairing of chocolate and orange makes these moist, fudgy squares absolutely irresistible. They are a great dessert for a party, as they can be made the day before and simply warmed up and served with orange ice cream or lightly whipped cream. They also freeze well for a few weeks.

Makes 16

175g (6oz) dark chocolate (55–62% cocoa solids), roughly chopped
175g (6oz) butter, cubed
25g (1oz) cocoa powder
3 eggs
225g (8oz) caster sugar
zest of 1 orange
100g (3½oz) plain flour
cocoa powder or icing sugar, for dusting

20cm (8in) square cake tin

1. Preheat the oven to 180°C (350°F) Gas mark 4. Grease the sides of the tin, and line the base and sides with baking parchment. Put the chocolate and butter in a heatproof bowl and sift in the cocoa powder. Put over a pan of gently simmering water until melted, making sure the base of the bowl doesn't touch the water, and stirring regularly. Remove the bowl from the heat.

2. In the bowl of a food processor, whisk the eggs, sugar and orange zest until light and fluffy. (Alternatively, put the ingredients in a large bowl and use an electric beater.) While continuing to whisk, add the chocolate mixture until well combined. Sift in the flour and fold in well.

3. Spoon the mixture into the prepared tin and bake for 20–25 minutes until it is dry on top but still slightly fudgy inside. Leave to cool in the tin on a wire rack and then cut into 16 squares. Dust with cocoa powder or icing sugar, if you like.

Choux cinnamon fingers

A super way to enjoy choux pastry, these light fingers are a little bit crisp and coated in sweet, crunchy cinnamon sugar – just divine.

Makes about 40

sunflower oil, for deep-
  frying
1 x quantity Choux Pastry
  (see page 240)
100g (3½oz) caster sugar
2 tsp ground cinnamon

piping bag with a 7mm
  (⅜in) star or plain nozzle
  or larger (see tip)

1. Heat the oil in a deep-fat fryer to 180°C (350°F), or use a large saucepan over a medium-high heat (test by frying a small cube of bread; it should brown in 40 seconds).

2. Put the choux pastry in the piping bag. Put the caster sugar in a bowl large enough to toss the choux fingers in, and add the cinnamon. Mix well together.

3. When the oil is up to temperature, gently pipe 4cm (1½in) lengths of choux pastry into the oil, but don't overcrowd the pan or the temperature will drop and the choux fingers will stick together.

4. Cook for 3–4 minutes until puffed and golden, then lift them out of the oil using a slotted spoon and drop them immediately into the cinnamon sugar. Toss them in the sugar, then put them on to a serving plate and serve straight away.

Tip: If you don't have a piping bag, you can just cut a corner off a plastic food bag and use that instead, or you can use a couple of teaspoons to spoon blobs of the choux pastry into the oil.

Pecan and cinnamon bakes

Traybakes were always one of my favourite things to make when I was a girl, as you can so easily vary the flavourings according to what you feel like that day. I would take them into school and treat all my friends, and they guessed years before I did that I would end up cooking for a living! This is one of my favourite flavour combinations – cinnamon, pecan and maple.

Makes 9

175g (6oz) butter, softened,
   plus extra for greasing
175g (6oz) soft light brown
   sugar
3 eggs
225g (8oz) plain flour
1 tsp baking powder
1½ tsp ground cinnamon
2 tbsp milk
100g (3½oz) pecan nuts,
   roughly chopped
4 tbsp maple syrup, for
   drizzling

20cm (8in) square cake tin
   with high sides

1. Preheat the oven to 180°C (350°F) Gas mark 4. Grease the base and sides of the tin, and line with baking parchment. Put the butter in a large bowl and cream it with a wooden spoon until soft, or use an electric beater on slow or a food processor. Add the sugar and beat until light and fluffy. Add the eggs one at a time, adding 1 tablespoon flour each time and beating well after each addition.

2. Sift in the remaining flour, the baking powder and cinnamon and fold in to combine, then stir in the milk. Spoon the mixture into the prepared tin and scatter the pecan nuts over the top.

3. Bake for 35–45 minutes until a skewer inserted into the centre comes out clean. While still warm, drizzle the maple syrup over the pecan nuts, allowing it to soak in. Cut into 9 squares and serve warm.

Apple and blackberry traybake

This delicious autumnal treat is great served warm as a dessert with softly whipped cream or with an afternoon cup of tea. Feel free to replace the blackberries with raspberries for a more summery flavour.

Makes 16

150g (5½oz) butter, softened, plus extra for greasing
150g (5½oz) caster sugar
2 eggs
100g (3½oz) plain flour
1 tsp vanilla extract
1 tsp baking powder
100g (3½oz) ground almonds
2 cooking apples, peeled, cored and finely diced
150g (5½oz) fresh or frozen blackberries

20cm (8in) square cake tin with high sides

1. Preheat the oven to 180°C (350°F) Gas mark 4. Grease the sides of the tin, and line the base with baking parchment. Put the butter in a large bowl and cream it with a wooden spoon until soft, or use an electric beater on slow or a food processor. Add the sugar and beat until light and fluffy.

2. Add the eggs, one at a time, adding 1 tablespoon flour each time and beating well after each addition, then add the vanilla extract and mix to combine. Sift the remaining flour and baking powder into another bowl. Add the ground almonds and stir together.

3. Fold the flour mixture into the butter mixture, then add the apples and fold to combine. Spoon the batter into the prepared tin, smooth the top using the back of the spoon, then scatter the blackberries over the top.

4. Bake for 40–50 minutes until a skewer inserted into the centre comes out clean and the sponge is nicely golden on top. Leave to cool in the tin on a wire rack for 2–3 minutes before cutting into squares and gently lifting out to serve.

Maple pecan slices

There may be a temptation to cut these into larger pieces, but a little definitely goes a long way as far as these superb slices go! They are rich and indulgent, and perfect with a strong coffee. They can be made well in advance and kept in the fridge until needed.

Makes 16 – 20

150g (5½oz) butter, cubed,
  plus extra for greasing
4 tbsp maple syrup
50g (1¾oz) soft light brown
  sugar
1 tsp vanilla extract
125g (4½oz) digestive
  biscuits
125g (4½oz) plain flour
50g (1¾oz) porridge oats
75g (2½oz) pecan nuts,
  roughly chopped
150g (5½oz) dark chocolate
  (55–62% cocoa solids),
  roughly chopped

20cm (8in) square cake tin

1. Preheat the oven to 180°C (350°F) Gas mark 4. Grease the side of the tin, and line the base with baking parchment. Put the butter, maple syrup, sugar and vanilla extract in a small saucepan over a low heat. Stir gently until the butter melts and the sugar dissolves. Remove from the heat.

2. Put the digestive biscuits in a food processor and pulse until they are reduced to fine crumbs. (Alternatively, put the biscuits in a plastic bag, tie the top and crush them with a rolling pin.) Tip into a large bowl.

3. Sift in the flour and add the oats and pecan nuts. Mix together well, then pour the melted butter mixture over the top and mix together until well combined.

4. Spoon the mixture into the prepared tin and press down with the back of a spoon so that the top is level. Bake for 14–16 minutes until lightly golden. Leave to cool in the tin on a wire rack.

5. Melt the chocolate in a heatproof bowl over a pan of gently simmering water, making sure the base of the bowl doesn't touch the water, and stirring regularly. Pour the melted chocolate over the cooled biscuit base and spread out evenly. Chill in the fridge for 45–60 minutes until set. Remove from the tin and transfer to a serving plate. Cut into 16–20 slices and serve.

Salted caramel peanut bars

OK, these are not technically a bake, but they've earned their place in the book by being just generally incredible! The lovely biscuity peanut base is topped with a thick layer of chocolate studded with peanuts and sprinkled with sea salt, which ties it all together.

Makes 18

100g (3½oz) butter, plus
extra for greasing
250g (9oz) digestive biscuits
100g (3½oz) soft light
brown sugar
250g (9oz) crunchy or
smooth peanut butter
200g (7oz) dark chocolate
(55–62% cocoa solids),
roughly chopped
150g (5½oz) tinned caramel,
or boiled condensed milk
(see tip)
30g (1¼oz) salted peanuts
a pinch of sea salt flakes

20cm (8in) square cake tin

1. Grease the base and sides of the tin and line with baking parchment. Put the butter in a small saucepan over a medium-low heat until melted. Put the digestive biscuits in a food processor and add the sugar. Pulse until the biscuits are reduced to fine crumbs. (Alternatively, put the biscuits in a plastic bag, tie the top and crush them with a rolling pin. Tip into a bowl and add the sugar.)

2. Add the melted butter and the peanut butter to the crushed biscuits and blend with the food processor, or mix with an electric beater, until they come together. Scrape down the sides of the food processor or bowl and mix again for a few seconds. Tip the mixture into the prepared tin and smooth it out using the back of the spoon. Put in the fridge for 30 minutes to chill.

3. Melt the chocolate in a heatproof bowl over a pan of gently simmering water, making sure the base of the bowl doesn't touch the water, and stirring regularly for a glossy finish. Pour the melted chocolate over the biscuit base in the tin.

4. Use a teaspoon to spoon the caramel over the chocolate topping in blobs, then scatter with the salted peanuts. Using a knife, or the handle of a teaspoon, swirl the mixture well to create a ripple effect, then scatter with a pinch of sea salt flakes. Return the mixture to the fridge for 30 minutes to chill and set, then lift it out of the tin and cut into 18 bars to serve.

Tip: If you are unable to buy tinned caramel, you can buy condensed milk and boil it in the tin, unopened, in a saucepan of water for 3 hours. Make sure that you leave it to cool in the tin before opening. I often boil a few at a time and keep them for another time, as they will keep for a year, or even more!

Chocolate and coconut flapjacks

These flapjacks are great to have on hand, especially if you know you might have friends popping in. They will happily keep for a few days in an airtight container, ready to be brought out with coffee at a moment's notice, and they freeze well, too. Cut into small squares, they make a great edible gift, and you could always dip them in some more dark chocolate and scatter them with a few coconut flakes to make them look even more appealing.

Makes 24 – 28

350g (12oz) butter, softened
2 generous tbsp golden
  syrup
175g (6oz) soft light brown
  sugar
75g (2½oz) plain flour
375g (13oz) porridge oats
75g (2½oz) dark chocolate
  (55–62% cocoa solids),
  roughly chopped
50g (1¾oz) desiccated
  coconut

25 x 38cm (10 x 15in) Swiss
  roll tin

1. Preheat the oven to 180°C (350°F) Gas mark 4. Line the Swiss roll tin with baking parchment. Put the butter, golden syrup and sugar in a large saucepan over a medium heat. Bring to a simmer and stir, allowing the butter to melt. When the mixture is smooth and well mixed, take the pan off the heat.

2. Add the flour, oats, chocolate and coconut, and mix until combined. The chocolate will melt as you mix, and the mixture will take on a lovely glossy chocolately appearance.

3. Spread the mixture in the tin and smooth the top using the back of the spoon. Bake for 15–25 minutes until golden. While still warm, cut into squares or fingers of any size you like. Leave to cool completely in the tin on a wire rack, then gently lift out of the tin to serve.

Oat and quinoa bars

These fruity, oaty cereal bars are great for a shot of energy on the go. They are packed with good, wholesome things, including protein-packed quinoa, and so are satisfying – they make a great after-sports snack. For an extra treat you could even drizzle these with a really dark 'healthy' chocolate with at least 70 per cent cocoa solids.

Makes 24

200g (7oz) red or white
  quinoa
100g (3½oz) rolled oats
250g (9oz) honey
150g (5½oz) crunchy or
  smooth peanut butter
50g (1¾oz) brown sugar
25g (1oz) coconut oil
¼ tsp salt
100g (3½oz) dried fruit
  such as raisins, sultanas,
  dried cranberries
50g (1¾oz) desiccated
  coconut

20cm (8in) square cake tin;
  baking tray

1. Preheat the oven to 180°C (350°F) Gas mark 4. Line the base and sides of the tin with baking parchment. Spread the quinoa and oats evenly over the baking tray and bake for 4 minutes, then take the tray out of the oven and stir the mixture. Spread it out again and return it to the oven for another 4 minutes.

2. Put the honey in a saucepan over a medium-low heat and add the peanut butter, sugar, coconut oil and salt. Melt together and stir until smooth, then tip into a large bowl.

3. Add the roasted quinoa and oats, the dried fruit and coconut. Mix well, then tip into the cake tin and spread out evenly. Bake for 15–20 minutes until golden on top. Leave to cool in the tin on a wire rack, then cut into 24 bars.

Persian almond bites with rosewater syrup

I think of these bites as a sort of cakey version of baklava. They encapsulate some of those favourite flavours of the Middle East, with almonds and rose, and I have kept them in their traditional diamond shape, too. They can be made in advance, as they keep very well in an airtight container, and are just as good to serve with strong coffee as their filo-based counterparts.

Makes 28 – 32

150g (5½oz) butter,
  softened
150g (5½oz) caster sugar
4 eggs, lightly beaten
250g (9oz) ground almonds
½ tsp baking powder

For the almond topping

100g (3½oz) almonds, with
  skins, roughly chopped
2 tbsp soft light brown
  sugar
1 tsp ground cardamom

For the rosewater syrup

100g (3½oz) sugar
4 tsp rosewater

33 x 23cm (13 x 9in) Swiss
  roll tin

1. Preheat the oven to 180°C (350°F) Gas mark 4. Line the base and sides of the tin with baking parchment. Put the butter in a large bowl and cream it with a wooden spoon until soft, or use an electric beater on slow or a food processor. Add the sugar and beat until light and fluffy.

2. Add the eggs and continue mixing until combined. Fold in the ground almonds and the baking powder. Spoon the almond sponge mixture into the prepared tin and smooth the top using the back of the spoon.

3. Put the almond topping ingredients in a small bowl and mix together, then spoon this over the almond sponge in the tin, Bake for 20–25 minutes until lightly golden and springy to the touch.

4. To make the rosewater syrup, put the sugar in a small saucepan and add 200ml (7fl oz) water, then stir over a medium heat until the sugar has dissolved. Take the pan off the heat and stir in the rosewater.

5. Using a skewer or a cocktail stick, prick the baked sponge all over. Slowly and gently pour the rosewater syrup all over the top so that the sponge absorbs all the syrup.

6. Leave to cool in the tin on a wire rack, then carefully lift the baking parchment containing the almond sponge on to a chopping board. Cut lengthways into strips 4cm

(1½in) wide, then, starting at one corner, cut lengths
4cm (1½in) wide diagonally across the sponge to create
diamond-shaped 'bites' and a few triangles from the
corners. Of course, you can cut into squares instead, but
the cakes look more authentic when cut into diamond
shapes. Serve with a strong coffee or a
cup of tea and enjoy!

Savoury Bakes

Smoked salmon, tomato and dill tart

Rich and flavoursome, this deliciously luxurious tart has a buttery, crumbly base and a creamy filling. Feel free to replace the dill with fennel or chives, if you prefer.

Serves 6 – 8

1 x quantity Shortcrust
    Pastry (see page 234)
25g (1oz) butter
1 large onion, finely
    chopped
3 eggs and 2 egg yolks
450ml fresh double cream
4 ripe tomatoes, peeled
    (see tip), deseeded and
    chopped
1 tbsp chopped dill leaves
300g (11oz) smoked salmon,
    cut into 1cm (½in) pieces
sea salt and freshly ground
    black pepper

23cm (9in) loose-bottomed
    tart tin with 2cm (¾in)
    sides

1. Use the pastry to line the tin and bake blind as explained on page 236.

2. To make the filling for the tart, melt the butter in a saucepan, then add the onion and some salt and pepper, cover with a lid and sweat over a gentle heat for 8–10 minutes until completely softened but not browned. Remove from the heat and leave to cool.

3. Put the eggs and egg yolks in a large bowl and add the cream, then whisk together. Stir in the cooked onion along with the chopped tomatoes, dill and smoked salmon. Season to taste with salt and pepper, then carefully pour the filling into the tart case, making sure that all the ingredients are evenly distributed.

4. Bake for 35 minutes or until golden on top and just set in the centre. Leave the tart to stand for 2–3 minutes before removing it from the tin, and serve either warm or at room temperature.

Tip: To peel the tomatoes, use a sharp knife to score a cross in the base of each one, cutting through the skin. Put the tomatoes in a bowl and cover with boiling water, then leave them in the water for 10–15 seconds. Drain and rinse in cold water, then peel away the skin – it should come away very easily.

Smoked haddock, salmon and prawn pie

I find few foods as comforting as a warm plate of fish pie. Whether topped with crisp buttery pastry or soft soothing mashed potato, I adore cutting that first piece, breaking the crust to reveal the delicious steaming-hot filling beneath. A good topping is just as important as your filling. Feel free to ring the changes by swapping the smoked haddock, salmon and prawns for other fish, either smoked or fresh.

Serves 6 – 8

50g (1¾oz) butter
1 onion, finely sliced
900ml (1½ pints) milk
300g (11oz) skinned smoked haddock, cut into 3cm (1¼in) pieces
300g (11oz) skinned salmon, cut into 3cm (1¼in) pieces
16 raw prawns or langoustines
50g (1¾oz) plain flour, plus extra for dusting
100ml (3½fl oz) fresh double cream
2 tbsp chopped fresh parsley leaves
275g (10oz) Puff (see page 238) or flaky pastry, thawed if frozen
1 egg
salt and freshly ground black pepper

20 x 30cm (8 x 12in) pie dish; small pastry cutters in shapes (optional)

1. Put 25g (1oz) of the butter in a wide saucepan over a medium heat and, when foaming, add the onion. Season with salt and pepper and cook, stirring occasionally, for 8–10 minutes until the onion is soft and very light golden.

2. Add the milk and bring to the boil, then reduce the heat to a simmer. Add the haddock, salmon and prawns and poach in the milk for 2–3 minutes until just cooked, then remove from the heat. Drain the mixture, reserving the milk, and put the fish in a bowl. Leave to cool. Preheat the oven to 230°C (450°F) Gas mark 8.

3. Melt the remaining butter in the saucepan over a medium heat, then add the flour and cook for 1 minute, stirring constantly.

4. Pour in the reserved milk and bring the mixture to the boil, whisking constantly to create a smooth sauce. Remove from the heat and stir in the cream and the parsley. Taste and adjust the seasoning.

5. Put the fish in the pie dish, then cover with the sauce. Roll out the pastry on a lightly floured work surface until 5mm (¼in) thick and a little over 1cm (½in) larger than the top of the pie dish and rim. Cut off a 1cm (½in) band of pastry, which you will use to line to the rim of the dish.

6. Beat the egg with a pinch of salt to make an egg wash and use to brush the rim of the pie dish, then lay the band of pastry over it and meet the ends together, cutting off the excess.

7. Brush the pastry band with egg wash, then put the large piece of pastry over the pie. Press down the edges so that the two layers of pastry are stuck together. If you like, roll out any scraps of pastry and cut out shapes for decorating the pie, then stick them to the pastry top using egg wash.

8. Using a skewer, make a hole in the centre of the pastry for steam to escape, then brush the top of the pastry with the beaten egg wash to glaze. Bake for 10 minutes, then reduce the temperature to 190°C (375°F) Gas mark 5 and cook for 20 minutes or until the pastry is golden brown and the filling hot and bubbling. Serve.

Variation: To make a potato-topped fish pie, preheat the oven to 180°C (350°F) Gas mark 4. Boil 1.25kg (2lb 12oz) scrubbed, unpeeled floury potatoes in a saucepan of water with a good pinch of salt for 10 minutes, then pour out all but 4cm (1½in) of the water. Continue to cook the potatoes over a very low heat. (Don't stick a knife into them as the skins will break and they will disintegrate.) Continue to cook for another 20–30 minutes until a skewer goes in easily. Drain the potatoes, and peel them while they are still hot, then put them into a bowl to mash immediately until smooth. Bring 175ml (6fl oz) milk, or 140ml (4¾fl oz) milk and 60ml (2fl oz) fresh single or double cream to the boil in a small saucepan. Add 30g (11/4oz) butter and some salt and pepper. Add most of this mixture to the potatoes with 1 egg yolk, and stir to a smooth consistency, adding more as needed depending on how dry the potatoes are. Spread the potato over the pie filling in the dish, making sure to go close to the edge of the dish. Dot the top with a few small knobs of butter, then cook in the oven for 30 minutes or until golden and bubbling hot.

Aubergine, mint and feta pashtida

A pashtida is an Israeli dish, similar to a quiche. You can vary the fillings, but I have stuck with a Middle Eastern theme here with a lovely combination of aubergine and mint, and finished it with salty feta.

Serves 6–8

1½ x quantity Shortcrust
    Pastry (see page 234)
4 tbsp extra virgin olive oil
2 red onions, sliced
1 aubergine, cut in half
    lengthways and sliced
3 eggs
200ml (7fl oz) fresh double
    cream
1 handful of mint leaves,
    chopped
200g (7oz) feta cheese
sea salt and freshly ground
    black pepper

22cm (8½in) loose-
    bottomed tart tin

1. Use the pastry to line the tin, trim and bake blind as explained on page 236.

2. Heat 2 tablespoons of the oil in a large frying pan over a high heat, then add the onions and season with a little salt and pepper. Cook for 5–8 minutes until wilted and tender, then remove the onions to a plate. Put the pan back on the heat and add the remaining olive oil. Add the aubergine, then cook for 10 minutes until tender and a little golden around the edges, tossing the pan regularly.

3. Put the eggs in a bowl and add the cream and mint, then whisk together. Stir in the cooked onion and aubergine.

4. Pour into the baked pastry shell and crumble the feta cheese over the top. Bake for 30–40 minutes until golden brown and just set in the centre.

French onion tart

This delicious tart is packed with caramelised onions and the scent of fresh thyme. It is wonderful paired with a tomato chutney and some green salad. Enjoy it warm from the oven, or at room temperature.

Serves 6 – 8

1½ x quantity Shortcrust
  Pastry (see page 234)
25g (1oz) butter
1 tbsp extra virgin olive oil
500g (1lb 2oz) onions,
  sliced
1 garlic clove, crushed
4 thyme sprigs, leaves
  chopped
4 eggs
200ml (7fl oz) fresh double
  cream
sea salt and freshly ground
  black pepper

22cm (8½in) tart tin

1. Preheat the oven to 180°C (350°F) Gas mark 4. Roll out the shortcrust pastry to fit the tart tin, then trim it and bake it blind as explained on page 236.

2. While the pastry is cooking, heat the butter and oil in a saucepan over a medium heat, then add the onions, garlic and thyme, and season with salt and pepper. Cook over a medium-low heat for 20–30 minutes, stirring regularly and scraping the bottom of the pan, until the onions are very tender and golden in colour.

3. Put the eggs and the cream in a bowl and whisk well, then season with salt and pepper. Spread the caramelised onion mixture over the base of the pastry. Pour in the egg mixture, then bake in the centre of the oven for 30–40 minutes until light golden brown and just set in the centre.

4. Leave the tart to cool in the tin on a wire rack for 10 minutes before taking it out of the tin and serving. Enjoy it warm or at room temperature.

Spanish cheese, honey and thyme tarts

This recipe gets its inspiration from the delicious flavour of Manchego cheese that the Spanish love to drizzle with honey and sometimes sprinkle with thyme. I've put these all together on puff pastry to make gorgeous little tarts, just right for lunch or a light supper with a green salad. If you can't find Manchego, use a hard cheese that's got great flavour.

Makes 4

1 x quantity Puff Pastry (see page 238)
flour, for dusting
1 egg
150g (5½oz) rind-removed Manchego cheese or other hard, matured cheese (I love to use my local Toons Bridge Dairy cacio occhiato), cut into 2mm (⅟₁₆in) slices
4 tsp thyme leaves
2–3 tsp honey

baking sheet

1. Preheat the oven to 200°C (400°F) Gas mark 6. Line the baking sheet with baking parchment. Roll out the pastry on a lightly floured work surface to 22 x 35cm (8½ x 14in).

2. Cut the rectangle in half lengthways and then in half widthways to make 4 smaller rectangles, each about 11 x 18cm (4¼ x 7in). (Alternatively, you can make 4 round tarts: roll the pastry into a square instead of a rectangle and cut 4 circles about 14cm (5½in) in diameter – I use a saucer for this.)

3. Dust off the excess flour on top of the pastry, then flip the pastry pieces over and dust off again. I flip them over after cutting for a better puff around the edges. Using a small sharp knife, score an 8mm (⅜in) frame all round the edge, cutting two-thirds of the way through the pastry. Put the pastry pieces on the prepared baking sheet.

4. Whisk the egg with the pinch of salt to make an egg wash, then brush the egg wash over the frame, not going over the edges. Inside the frame, lay down the slices of cheese, making sure to cover the whole surface of the pastry inside the frame. Scatter ½ teaspoon of the thyme leaves over the cheese in each pastry.

5. Bake for 10–15 minutes until the pastry is puffed and golden. Remove from the oven and put on warm plates, then drizzle the honey thinly over the top of each tart. Scatter the remaining thyme leaves over the top, and serve.

Buttery chicken and mushroom puff pastry parcels with hollandaise sauce

Gorgeously buttery puff pastry is the perfect casing for these chicken and mushroom parcels. They make great use of leftover roast chicken (or turkey after the big Christmas meal), as you can put them, uncooked, into the freezer for another day if you don't fancy chicken two days in a row! This recipe was inspired by great friends of ours, who serve something like these at their annual post-Christmas party.

Serves 8

25g (1oz) butter, plus 5g (⅛oz)
2 tbsp finely chopped shallot
250g (9oz) button mushrooms, cut in half and finely sliced
250g (9oz) cooked chicken, cut into 1cm (½in) cubes
175ml (6fl oz) gravy or juices from the roast chicken, or chicken stock
175ml (6fl oz) fresh double cream, plus ½ tbsp
2 tsp chopped fresh thyme leaves
2 tsp chopped fresh chives
5g (⅛ oz) plain flour, plus extra for dusting
675g (1lb 7oz) Puff Pastry (see page 238), thawed if frozen
1 egg
sea salt and freshly ground black pepper

1. Melt half the 25g (1oz) butter in a wide saucepan over a medium heat. Allow it to foam, then add the shallot and season with salt and pepper. Cover with a lid, reduce the heat to low and sweat the shallot for 4–5 minutes until tender. Tip the shallot out of the pan on to a plate.

2. Return the pan to a high heat and add the second half of the butter. Once it melts and foams, add the mushrooms and toss for 2–3 minutes until wilted and almost golden, then season with salt and pepper. Add the chicken and toss with the mushrooms for 1–2 minutes until golden around the edges, then return the shallot to the pan and pour in the gravy and the 175ml (6fl oz) cream.

3. Bring to a gentle boil, then continue to simmer for 2 minutes. Add the herbs and taste the sauce; it should have good flavour. If it is still a bit weak, boil it, uncovered, for another 2 minutes until the flavour is good.

4. Melt the 5g (⅛oz) butter in a small saucepan over a medium-high heat. Allow it to foam, then add the flour and cook to make a roux, stirring regularly, for 1 minute or until paler in appearance and sandy in consistency.

2 egg yolks
115g (4oz) butter, cut into
   1cm (½in) cubes
a squeeze of lemon juice

baking sheet

5. Make a little well in the centre of the pan with the chicken mixture so that there is just sauce and no chicken or mushrooms. Put the roux in the centre and turn the heat down, then whisk the roux into the sauce so that it thickens slightly. Taste for seasoning and take off the heat to cool. To speed up cooling, pour the mixture out on to a plate.

6. Roll out the puff pastry on a lightly floured work surface, and also dust the top of the pastry with flour. Keep rolling as evenly as possible, making sure to keep it floured underneath so that it doesn't stick to the surface, until it is 3mm (⅛in) thick. Put the pastry on a baking sheet and pop it into the fridge to chill for 20 minutes before cutting.

7. Roll the pastry again (as it will probably have shrunk a little and thickened slightly) until no thicker than 3mm (⅛in) thick. Cut 8 circles 15cm (6in) in diameter (you can use a small saucer of that measurement). Save the scraps for Cheese and Rosemary Twists (see page 170), or re-roll the scraps if you need to for the 8 circles.

8. Put a circle on the lightly floured worktop and put 1 generous tablespoon (but not too heaped), of the chicken mixture on one half of the circle, making sure to leave a border of at least 1cm (½in). Beat the egg with the ½ tablespoon cream, then brush this egg wash around the edge of the pastry and fold the parcel over so that you have a semi-circular shape.

9. Using the prongs of a fork, stamp all round the curved edge to ensure the edges stick, then turn over and do the same on the other side. These pastries can be placed on their sides to bake, once brushed with the egg wash, but I like to arrange them so that they sit up on the fold and the half-moon shape is going over the top, like a little purse. Brush all exposed sides with egg wash, then put in the fridge for 15 minutes. This chilling will trap all the lovely butter inside the pastry so that it doesn't escape during baking. They can also be covered and frozen for up to 3 months.

10. Preheat the oven to 210°C (415°F) Gas mark 6½. Put the parcels on the baking sheet, well spaced apart, and bake for 15–20 minutes, until golden and hot on the inside. If you wish to test for doneness, you can stick a metal skewer into the centre of one of the parcels, leave it in for a few seconds, then take it out. It should be good and hot.

Continued...

11. While the parcels are cooking, make the hollandaise sauce. Put the egg yolks in a small heavy-based saucepan over a low heat and add 1 tablespoon water. Immediately add two cubes of the butter to the pan and start to whisk the mixture to blend the butter into the egg yolks. Repeat with two more cubes of butter as soon as the first two are mixed in. The pan must not get too hot or the mixture will scramble or split. Ensure that it doesn't overheat by regularly holding your hands around the sides of the pan; if it's too hot to hold, it's too hot for the eggs. Move the pan off and on the heat regularly to prevent it overheating and never leave the sauce unattended over the heat.

12. When all the butter has been added, you should have a rich, yellow, thickened sauce. Take it off the heat and add the lemon juice to flavour. It shouldn't require salt if you've used salted butter; however, if you've used unsalted butter, add salt to taste. Use the sauce straight away, or you can keep it warm (see tip). Serve the pastries warm with the hollandaise sauce.

Tip: To keep hollandaise sauce warm, you can use a vacuum flask (which is very convenient if you're taking the sauce to someone's house). I prefer to pour it into a heatproof jug, and put it in a saucepan containing steaming-hot but not boiling water to keep it warm. Heat up the water when it cools, but beware, because the sauce can still scramble or split at this stage. If you allow the sauce to cool and then heat it up, it will split, so temperature control is crucial, as for any of the emulsified-butter sauces. If it's been keeping warm for a while longer than 20 minutes it might thicken a little, in which case you'll need to add a small splash of water to thin it out.

Asparagus, tomato and spring onion tart

Gorgeously light yet luxurious, this tart is made with a crumbly short pastry. Serve barely warm or at room temperature with a fresh green salad on the side and a chilled glass of something white if you wish.

Serves 6 – 8

1 x quantity Shortcrust
    Pastry (see page 234)
1 tbsp olive oil
200g (7oz) spring onions,
    finely sliced
200g (7oz) asparagus spears,
    trimmed
4 eggs
350ml (12fl oz) fresh double
    cream
150g (5½oz) cherry
    tomatoes, cut in half
25g (1oz) Parmesan cheese,
    finely grated
sea salt and freshly ground
    black pepper

23cm (9in) loose-bottomed
    tart tin with 2cm (¾in)
    sides

1. Use the pastry to line the tin, trim and bake blind as explained on page 236.

2. To make the tart filling, heat the olive oil in a small saucepan, add the spring onions and cook over a low heat until soft. Bring a pan of water to the boil and add a pinch of salt, drop in the asparagus, cover and return to the boil, then remove the lid and boil, uncovered, for 3–4 minutes until it is just cooked. Drain, and cut the asparagus diagonally into 3cm (1¼in) pieces.

3. Whisk the eggs in a bowl, add the cream and the spring onions, and season with salt and pepper. Pour this filling into the cooked pastry shell, still in the tin. Drop the asparagus into the tart and arrange the cherry tomatoes on top, then sprinkle the Parmesan cheese over the top. Carefully put the tart into the oven and cook for 20–30 minutes until it is just set in the centre. Serve out of the tin, hot or at room temperature.

Spiced lamb pasties

*There are so many wonderful flavours packed into these pasties –
from Worcestershire sauce and English mustard to Indian spices, such
as coriander and cumin. It is this masterful blending of cuisine culture
that characterises modern European food, and makes it so exciting.*

Makes 12 – 15

225g (8oz) plain flour, plus
    extra for dusting
½ tsp ground turmeric
¼ tsp ground black pepper
1 egg, beaten
75g (2½oz) butter, cubed
sea salt freshly ground black
    pepper

For the filling

1 tsp coriander seeds
1 tsp cumin seeds
2 tbsp olive oil
150g (5½oz) onions, chopped
2 garlic cloves, chopped
1cm (½in) root ginger, peeled
    and finely grated
200g (7oz) minced lamb
1 tbsp tomato purée
1 tsp English mustard
1 tsp Worcestershire sauce
100g (3½oz) frozen peas
1 tbsp chopped mint leaves
1 egg, beaten

baking sheet

1. Put the coriander and cumin seeds for the filling in a dry pan over a medium-high heat, and toast for 30–60 seconds until they are slightly darker in colour and just starting to smoke. Crush them straight away using a spice grinder or a mortar and pestle. Set aside.

2. To make the pastry, sift the flour into a large bowl and stir in the turmeric, pepper and a pinch of salt. Make a well in the centre and add the egg.

3. Put the butter in a saucepan and add 100ml (3½fl oz) water. Heat over a medium heat, stirring occasionally, until the butter melts, then allow the mixture to come to a rolling boil.

4. Pour the hot liquid into the flour and stir with a wooden spoon to mix. Spread the mixture out on a large plate using the wooden spoon and leave to cool for 15 minutes, then wrap in cling film and chill in the fridge for 30 minutes or until firm.

5. To make the filling, heat the oil in a saucepan over a medium heat and add the onions, garlic and ginger. Season with salt and pepper, and cook until the onions are soft and slightly golden.

6. Add the coriander and cumin to the pan, followed by the lamb, tomato purée, mustard and Worcestershire sauce. Cook over a medium-low heat for 15 minutes or until the lamb is cooked and some of the liquid has been reduced. Add the peas for the last 2 minutes of cooking. Add the mint, then season to taste and leave to cool. Preheat the oven to 220°C (425°F) Gas mark 7.

. Roll out the dough on a lightly
floured work surface to 2mm (1/16in)
thick. Using a small saucer or similar,
cut the dough into 10cm (4in) circles.

. Lay 1 generous tablespoon of the mixture on
one half of a circle and brush the edge of the
other half with the beaten egg, then fold it over to
form a semi-circle. Pinch the edges together to seal,
making sure that there is no air trapped inside, and
mark the edges with a fork. Repeat until all the circles and
filling are used up.

. Brush the tops with beaten egg and put on the baking
sheet. Bake for 15–20 minutes until golden and a
skewer inserted into the centre of each comes
out hot. Serve hot or at room temperature.

Baked samosas with chilli and mint dip

Delicious warm from the oven, these samosas are also great for livening up a picnic. They are baked and not fried, using filo pastry rather than the softer samosa dough. Serve with the hot chilli dip on the side and let people decide how brave they are feeling!

Makes 12

300g (11oz) sweet potatoes, peeled and cut into chunks
1 tbsp olive oil
1 onion, chopped
200g (7oz) spinach leaves without stalks, chopped
1 tsp sumac
100g (3½oz) peas, frozen and thawed
6 sheets of filo pastry, thawed if frozen
50g (1¾oz) butter, melted
sea salt and freshly ground black pepper

For the green chilli and mint dip

150g (5½oz) caster sugar
75ml (2¼fl oz) white wine vinegar
3 green chillies, deseeded and finely chopped
6 large mint sprigs, leaves finely chopped

baking sheet

1. Boil the sweet potatoes in a large saucepan of water for 10 minutes or until tender. Drain in a colander and return to the pan. Use a potato masher to mash the potatoes. Set aside.

2. Heat the oil in a large, wide saucepan over a medium heat and cook the onion with some salt and pepper for 5–10 minutes until tender and a little golden around the edges. Add the spinach and the sumac, and cook until the spinach has wilted.

3. Add the cooked sweet potato and the peas, and mix thoroughly. Adjust the seasoning, then leave to cool. Preheat the oven to 200°C (400°F) Gas mark 6.

4. Take 1 sheet of filo pastry and lay it out flat. Keep the remaining sheets covered with a damp, clean tea towel to ensure they don't dry out. Brush the filo sheet all over with the melted butter and add another sheet. Brush with melted butter, then cut into 4 long rectangles.

5. Put 1 tablespoon of filling in the bottom right-hand corner of a rectangle, then fold over the pastry, brushing the unbuttered sides with butter as you go and sealing the edges to make a triangle. Keep folding the pastry over, brushing with butter, until it forms a complete triangle.

6. Repeat with the remaining filo pastry until you have 12 samosas. Put the samosas on the baking sheet and bake for 12–15 minutes, or until golden brown.

7. Meanwhile, to make the dip, put the sugar and vinegar in a small saucepan over a medium-low heat until the sugar is dissolved. Add the chillies and mint, and mix thoroughly. Serve the dip with the hot samosas.

Knish dumplings

Originally from Eastern Europe, knish dumplings were the perfect street food: with their delicious fillings safely encased in dough, they were great for eating on the go. Mine are bite-sized, so they are handy as snacks or for entertaining.

Makes 16

250g (9oz) plain flour, plus
    extra for dusting
60ml (2fl oz) sunflower oil
½ tsp salt
1 egg yolk, beaten
tomato relish, to serve

For the filling

500g (1lb 2oz) floury
    potatoes, peeled and cut
    into chunks
15g (½oz) butter
½ onion
100g (3½oz) kale leaves,
    stalks removed, chopped
1 garlic clove, crushed
1 tbsp chopped fresh chives
50g (1¾oz) Cheddar cheese,
    grated
sea salt and freshly ground
    black pepper

baking sheet

1. To make the filling, boil the potatoes in a large saucepan of water for 15–20 minutes or until tender. Drain in a colander and return to the pan. Use a potato masher to mash the potatoes.

2. Melt the butter in a large non-stick frying pan over a medium heat until foaming. Add the onion and cook for 5–8 minutes until softened and starting to brown around the edges.

3. Add the kale and garlic, and cook for a further 3–4 minutes until the kale is tender. Stir in the mashed potatoes, the chives and cheese, then season with salt and pepper, and set aside to cool. Preheat the oven to 180°C (350°F) Gas mark 4. Line the baking sheet with baking parchment.

4. To make the pastry, put the flour, oil, salt and 100ml (3½fl oz) water into a food processor with a K (multipurpose) attachment. Mix on a slow speed for 1–2 minutes until the dough leaves the sides of the bowl. Alternatively, mix the ingredients together in a large bowl using a wooden spoon or an electric beater, then knead by hand for 3 minutes or until smooth.

5. Tip the dough out on to a floured work surface and roll out into a 30 x 30cm (12 x 12in) square about 3mm (⅛in) thick. Cut in half so that you have 2 rectangles. Put the potato and kale mixture in a sausage-like shape lengthways all the way down the centre of each rectangle.

6. Fold the pastry over the top and seal with the beaten egg yolks. Cut each of the cylinders into 8 pieces. With floured hands, pick up each piece and pull the pastry around to seal on the bottom to form an open-topped dumpling. Put the dumplings on to the prepared baking sheet cut-side up. Brush with the remaining egg and bake for 20–25 minutes until golden brown. Serve hot with tomato relish, if you wish.

Pâte aux pommes de terre

Dauphinoise potatoes were the height of indulgence until I met Eric, a French photographer with whom I worked, who told me about pâté au pommes de terre. These essentially take dauphinoise potatoes and put them into a puff-pastry case. Simply, wow!

Serves 6 – 8

1kg (2lb 4oz) potatoes, unpeeled
375g (13oz) Puff Pastry (see page 238), thawed if frozen
flour, for dusting
200ml (7fl oz) fresh double cream
1 egg yolk, beaten
½ tsp freshly grated nutmeg
2 tsp fresh thyme leaves, chopped
1 tsp salt
½ tsp freshly ground black pepper

baking tray

1. Line the baking tray with baking parchment. Boil the potatoes in a large saucepan of water for 20–30 minutes or until just tender. Cool, then remove the skins and cut into 5mm (¼in) slices. Put to one side. Preheat the oven to 200°C (400°F) Gas mark 6.

2. Roll out the puff pastry on a lightly floured work surface to a 25 x 40cm (10 x 16in) rectangle, 4mm (⅛in) thick, and trim around the edges. Flip the pastry over and put on to the prepared baking tray.

3. Using a sharp knife, score a 2cm (¾in) frame all round the edge (like a picture frame) cutting two-thirds of the way through the pastry, then score all over the central rectangle of pastry with a skewer or the tip of a sharp knife, at about 2cm (¾in) intervals.

4. Put the cream in a large bowl and add the egg yolk, nutmeg, thyme, salt and black pepper. Mix well, then add the potatoes and coat them in the cream mixture.

5. Brush the frame of the pastry with the beaten egg yolk. Put the potatoes into the centre of the tart, arranging them so that they overlap in lines, and pour the cream mixture over to cover evenly. Bake the tart for 30–40 minutes, or until golden and just set in the centre. Cut into slices to serve.

Bite-sized Yorkshire puddings with mustard sausages

Things always taste better in miniature, so not many people will be able to refuse this dinner favourite shrunk into perfect bite-sized pieces! It's a favourite for parties.

Makes 24

125g (4½oz) plain flour
4 eggs
300ml (11fl oz) milk
50ml (1¾fl oz) olive oil or
  sunflower oil
24 cocktail sausages
2 tbsp grainy mustard
salt
tomato relish or chutney,
  to serve

24-hole petit-four tray

1. Sift the flour and a pinch of salt into a bowl and make a well in the centre. Add the eggs and start whisking in the centre while also pouring in the milk. Continue to whisk, slowly drawing in the flour from the sides. Whisk until smooth, then transfer to a large jug. Cover and leave to rest at room temperature for 1–2 hours, or overnight if you prefer.

2. Preheat the oven to 200°C (400°F) Gas mark 6. Divide the oil between the 24 holes of the petit-four tray and put in the oven until smoking hot.

3. Coat the sausages with mustard. Remove the tray from the oven and pour the batter evenly into the 24 cups. Pop a coated sausage in the centre of each and bake for 20 minutes or until the puddings are well risen and the sausages are golden brown. Serve hot with tomato relish or chutney, if you wish.

Pea and cream cheese madeleines

Madeleines, those delicate shell-shaped French cakes, can also be delicious as a savoury bake, and are great for snacks if you don't feel like something sweet. These are made with peas and cream cheese, but there is an omnivore's variation below. This traditional madeleine recipe uses yeast.

Makes 12

175g (6oz) frozen petits pois, thawed
1–2 tbsp flour, as needed for dusting
100g (3½oz) cream cheese
zest of 1 small lemon
3 eggs
25ml (1fl oz) milk
25ml (1fl oz) fresh double cream
½ tsp salt
200g (7oz) plain flour
7g sachet of fast-action yeast
100g (3½oz) butter, melted, plus extra for greasing
2 tbsp finely chopped chives
freshly ground black pepper

12-hole madeleine tray

1. Put the peas in a colander and allow any moisture to drip away, then transfer them to a plate and dust them with a little flour, rolling them to coat them well. This will ensure that they stay looking good during cooking.

2. Put the cream cheese in a bowl and add the lemon zest. Combine well. In another bowl, beat the eggs, milk, cream and salt using a whisk. Sift in the flour and add the yeast, then stir to mix well.

3. Pour in the warm melted butter and chives, and season with pepper. Mix again to obtain a smooth batter. Fold in the cream cheese mixture using a spatula. Cover with a tea towel and leave the dough to rest in a warm place for 30 minutes. Preheat the oven to 180°C (350°F), Gas mark 4. Grease the holes of the madeleine tray.

4. Gently fold the peas into the mixture using the spatula. Take a heaped tablespoonful of the mixture and use another spoon to scoop it into a madeleine cup. Repeat with the remaining mixture. Leave to stand for 5 minutes, then put into the oven and bake for 14–16 minutes, checking and turning the tray halfway through, until the madeleines are golden brown. Leave in the tin on a wire rack to cool slightly before eating warm or at room temperature.

Variation: You can fold in some finely chopped fried bacon lardons, smoked salmon or salami pieces instead of the peas, if you like.

Gougères

Made with choux pastry, these classic French cheese puffs make great party snacks. You can also use the mix for some other tasty variations (see below).

Makes 30 – 40

1 x quantity Choux Pastry
   (see page 240)
150g (5½oz) grated Gruyère
   cheese
¼ tsp ground nutmeg
½ tsp salt
1 egg, beaten
freshly ground black pepper

three baking sheets; piping
   bag and a 1cm (½in) plain
   nozzle

1. Preheat the oven to 180°C (350°F) Gas mark 4. Line the baking sheets with baking parchment. Make the choux pastry as explained on page 240, then stir in 100g (3½oz) of the cheese, the nutmeg, salt and a pinch of pepper.

2. Transfer the dough to the piping bag and pipe walnut-sized mounds on to the baking sheets, spaced well apart. Brush the tops of the choux pastry with the egg and scatter over the remaining grated cheese.

3. Bake for 15–20 minutes until golden brown and puffed up. Make sure that the gougères are cooked in the centre – you might have to eat one to find out!

Variations: You can add finely chopped chorizo, or cooked crispy bacon to the pastry mix, before cooking. These are also divine piped straight (without brushing with the egg and scattering with the extra cheese) into oil preheated to 180°C (350°F) (test by frying a small cube of bread; it should brown in 40 seconds). Cook for 4–5 minutes until golden brown and cooked in the centre.

Smoky paprika and thyme soufflé bites

These flavoursome bites are a great way to use up a neglected loaf of bread. I have used sweet-smoked paprika here, but you could easily opt for hot-smoked paprika if you would prefer a more punchy chilli spice than the aromatic flavour these have.

Makes about 60

80g (2¾oz) butter
100g (3½oz) extra-mature Cheddar cheese, finely grated
80g (2¾oz) crème fraîche
2 large eggs, separated
2 tsp sweet-smoked paprika
2 tsp dried thyme
500g (1lb 2oz) stale white bread, crusts removed and cut into 2cm (¾in) cubes
sea salt flakes, to sprinkle
sea salt and freshly ground black pepper

two baking sheets

1. Preheat the oven to 200°C (400°F) Gas mark 6. Line the baking sheets with baking parchment. Melt the butter in a saucepan over a medium-low heat, then add the cheese. Stir until melted, then stir in the crème fraîche. Remove the pan from the heat, stir in the egg yolks, paprika and thyme, and season with salt and pepper.

2. Put the egg whites into a clean, grease-free bowl and whisk with an electric beater until they form stiff peaks, or use a food processor. Working quickly, fold the egg whites into the mixture in the pan.

3. Dip the cubes of bread into the mixture to coat well, scraping off any excess on the edge of the pan, and lay them on the prepared baking sheets. Bake for 6 minutes. Take the baking sheets out of the oven and turn each bread cube over, then return them to the oven, switching the baking sheets around so that they brown evenly, and cook for another 6 minutes or until puffed and golden all over. Sprinkle with sea salt flakes and serve.

Cheese and thyme soufflés

For this soufflé recipe I use two cheeses: a hard one such as a Parmesan, Pecorino, Manchego or one of my favourites – Toons Bridge Dairy cacio occhiato cheese – and something a little bit softer, like a Cheddar or Gruyère. The combination of the two cheeses gives these soufflés a great depth of flavour and a lovely light texture. Use your favourite cheeses that are most like these in texture.

Soufflés are much more easy-going than one might think. They can be prepared right up to the point of baking and kept in the fridge for up to an hour, and they can even be frozen. Make sure to take them out of the fridge or the freezer and straight into the preheated oven on a hot baking sheet for baking. They will take longer to cook if they've been frozen. Or, if you wish, you can make the soufflés up to the point of whisking the egg whites and set the mixture aside in the fridge for a few hours. Very gently heat the cheese sauce to lukewarm before whisking the egg whites with the pinch of salt (don't add the salt until ready to whisk), keeping in mind that the egg yolks will scramble (split) if you don't reheat the mixture very carefully and gently.

Makes 6

20g (¾oz) butter, plus 10g (¼oz) butter, melted
20g (¾oz) plain flour
225ml (8fl oz) milk
3 eggs, separated
40g (1½oz) hard cheese such as Parmesan, Pecorino or Manchego, finely grated
40g (1½oz) Cheddar cheese or Gruyère, grated
1 generous tsp chopped thyme leaves
sea salt and freshly ground black pepper

baking sheet; 6 individual soufflé dishes or 6cm (2½in) ramekins

1. Preheat the oven to 200°C (400°F) Gas mark 6 and put a baking sheet in the centre of the oven with the lip at the back, or upturned so that the sheet is flat for when you slide out the soufflés as they cook. Brush the 10g (¼oz) melted butter around the inside of each soufflé dish.

2. Melt the 20g (¾oz) butter in a small saucepan over a low heat, then add the flour and cook for 1–2 minutes until pale golden to make a roux. Pour the milk into the pan, whisking constantly until the mixture boils and thickens; this might take 3 minutes. Remove from the heat and set aside, then whisk the egg yolks into the sauce.

3. Whisk the cheeses and thyme into the sauce, mixing them in well so that the cheese melts. Taste for seasoning; it should taste slightly more highly seasoned than you want the soufflé to be eventually, as the egg whites will dilute the flavour somewhat.

4. Put the egg whites in a clean, grease-free bowl, add a pinch of salt, and whisk with an electric beater until they form stiff peaks, or use a food processor. Using a spatula, roughly fold a quarter of the egg whites into the cheese sauce in the pan, then gently pour the cheese sauce mixture into the side of the bowl with the egg whites (not right on top of them), and lightly fold together, trying to keep as much air in the mix as possible.

5. Spoon the mixture into the prepared dishes to the top, levelling off using a palette knife. Using a piece of kitchen paper, wipe around the sides to clean the edges all the way round.

6. Put on the hot baking sheet in the oven, slightly spaced apart, and bake for 8–10 minutes until puffed, risen and golden brown on top. When you lightly press the centre of them they should have a gentle spring. Take them out as they're cooked and put the soufflés on warm plates to serve immediately.

Cayenne and sesame cheese swirls

Cayenne and sesame are a match made in heaven: spicy and nutty. Throw in buttery pastry and melted cheese, and don't expect them to hang around for more than about 10 minutes.

Makes 12

375g (13oz) Puff Pastry (see page 238), thawed if frozen
flour, for dusting
1 egg yolk
25g (1oz) Parmesan cheese, freshly grated
½ tsp cayenne pepper
25g (1oz) Cheddar cheese, grated
25g (1oz) mozzarella, grated
½ tsp sesame seeds
salt

baking sheet

1. Preheat the oven to 200°C (400°F) Gas mark 6. Line a baking sheet with baking parchment. Roll out the pastry on a lightly floured work surface to 25 x 40cm (10 x 16in). Brush off the excess flour.

2. Beat the egg yolk with a pinch of salt and 1 tablespoon water to make an egg wash. Brush the pastry with the egg wash. Mix together the Parmesan and cayenne pepper, then sprinkle it over the pastry.

3. Using both hands, tightly roll both long edges of the pastry towards each other to form two swirls that meet in the centre. Make sure the pastry is rolled tightly to ensure it doesn't unfold.

4. Cut the pastry into 12 even-sized slices. Put on the prepared baking sheet and press down slightly. Mix together the Cheddar and mozzarella, then sprinkle over the top of each pastry. Sprinkle with sesame seeds. Bake for 15–20 minutes until golden and cooked underneath. Serve warm or at room temperature.

Caramelised red onion swirls

These savoury palmiers containing a sweet red onion marmalade are great for parties, especially when served warm straight from the oven. Just assemble them and keep them in the fridge covered with cling film until guests arrive, then pop them in the oven for a few minutes so that they are served as fresh as can be.

Makes 16

500g (1lb 2oz) red onions, sliced
25g (1oz) redcurrant jelly
25g (1oz) demerara or light brown sugar
juice of 1 orange
125ml (4½fl oz) red wine
375g (13oz) Puff Pastry (see page 238), thawed if frozen
flour, for dusting
sea salt and freshly ground black pepper

two or three baking sheets

1. Preheat the oven to 200°C (400°F) Gas mark 6. Line the baking sheets with baking parchment. Put the onions in a large saucepan over a medium heat with the redcurrant jelly, sugar, orange juice and wine. Bring to the boil, then allow to simmer, uncovered, for 20–30 minutes until the onions are tender and the mixture has reduced. Season with salt and pepper, and set aside to cool.

2. Roll out the puff pastry on a lightly floured work surface into a 25 x 40cm (10 x 16in) rectangle, 4mm (⅛in) thick. Spread the filling evenly over the base, making sure that it is spread right to the edges. Starting from the long side, roll up into a Swiss-roll shape, then cut into 16 even slices.

3. Put the slices, cut-side up, on the prepared baking sheets spaced well apart, as they will spread during cooking. If you don't have enough baking sheets, cook them in batches. Cook the swirls for 15 minutes or until golden and cooked underneath. Leave to cool on a wire rack for 5 minutes before enjoying them while warm.

Sausage rolls with fennel

Basic party sausage rolls can be given such a simple makeover by adding a sprinkle of toasted fennel seeds. It's a wonderful flavour combination, and a great twist on a classic baking recipe.

Makes 16

2 tsp fennel seeds
375g (13oz) Puff Pastry
   (see page 238), thawed if
   frozen
400g (14oz) sausagemeat
1 egg yolk
sea salt and freshly ground
   black pepper

baking sheet

1. Put the fennel seeds in a small saucepan and toast over a medium-high heat for 30 seconds or until aromatic. Cool, then grind in a mortar and pestle. Preheat the oven to 200°C (400°F) Gas mark 6.

2. Roll the pastry into a 25 x 40cm (10 x 16in) rectangle, 4mm (⅛in) thick, then cut it in half lengthways. Put the sausagemeat in a large bowl and add half the toasted fennel seeds and some salt and pepper. Mix together well. You can fry a tiny piece to taste for seasoning, if you like, then adjust the seasoning for the mixture if necessary.

3. Mould the sausagemeat into 2 sausage shapes, 40cm (16in) long, and put one along the centre of each pastry rectangle.

4. Whisk the egg yolk in a small bowl with 1 tablespoon water and a pinch of salt to make an egg wash. Brush the egg wash around the edges of the pastry. Fold the pastry over on itself, and seal the edges with a fork.

5. Cut each pastry roll into 8 sausage rolls, and put on the baking sheet. Brush with the egg wash once more, and sprinkle the remaining fennel seeds over the top of each. Bake for 20 minutes or until a rich golden brown all over. Serve warm or cold.

Cheese and rosemary twists

These delicious little treats should come with a warning, as they can be completely addictive. They are perfect to enjoy with an aperitif. Puff-pastry scraps are ideal to use to make them, as long as they are laid carefully on top of each other, then rolled out with a dusting of flour on top and underneath.

Makes about 80

200g (7oz) Puff Pastry (see page 238)
flour, for dusting
50g (1¾oz) Parmesan cheese, finely grated
2 tsp finely chopped fresh rosemary leaves
1 egg
salt

baking sheet; pastry wheel (optional)

1. Preheat the oven to 200°C (400°F) Gas mark 6. Line a baking sheet with baking parchment. Roll out the pastry on a floured work surface to a 25 x 30cm (10 x 12in) rectangle, 3mm (⅛in) thick. Brush off the excess flour.

2. Put the cheese and rosemary in a bowl and mix together. Beat the egg with a pinch of salt and use this egg wash to brush over the pastry, then scatter with half the cheese mixture. Use the rolling pin to gently press the cheese into the pastry.

3. Turn the pastry over and repeat the egg washing, scattering with the cheese mix and gently pressing it into the pastry.

4. Cut the pastry into long strips 1cm (½in) wide, using a pastry wheel if you wish, and cut each strip into pieces 16cm (6¼in) long. Holding each end, twist each length and then put it on the prepared baking sheet. Bake for 8–10 minutes until puffed, golden and cooked through. Serve warm or at room temperature.

Desserts

Chocolate, fig and hazelnut panforte

Panforte is a rich, Italian cake containing dried fruit, although the addition of chocolate here is my personal twist. It's perfect to serve in small portions with an after-dinner coffee, and is also popular at Christmas. To make this look more festive, you could decorate it with gold leaf (now available in the baking sections of some supermarkets) or dust it with a snow of icing sugar.

Serves 16 – 20

25g (1oz) butter, cubed, plus extra for greasing
100g (3½oz) hazelnuts, toasted with skins, then skins removed (see page 245) and roughly chopped
100g (3½oz) almonds, toasted with skins and roughly chopped (see page 245)
125g (4½oz) dried figs, roughly chopped
50g (1¾oz) plain flour
zest of 1 orange
100g (3½oz) dark chocolate (55–62% cocoa solids), roughly chopped, or use dark chocolate drops
150g (5½oz) honey
75g (2½oz) soft light brown sugar
gold leaf or icing sugar, for dusting (optional)

20cm (8in) round springform cake tin; sugar thermometer

1. Preheat the oven to 150°C (300°F) Gas mark 2. Grease and line the base and side of the tin with baking parchment. Put the hazelnuts in the bowl of a food processor, then add the almonds and figs. Sift in the flour and add the orange zest and chocolate. Combine well until the nuts and fruit are roughly chopped.

2. Put the butter in a saucepan and add the honey and sugar, then set over a medium-low heat. Stir until the butter has melted, and then continue to heat for 5–10 minutes until the mixture is thick and syrupy, and a sugar thermometer reads 110–115°C (225–240°F) when inserted into the mixture. When it has reached this stage, remove the pan from the heat and immediately pour the mixture into the nut mixture.

3. Beat well until combined, then spoon the mixture into the prepared tin and flatten with the back of a spoon. Bake for 50–55 minutes until the cake feels firm in the centre. Remove from the oven and leave in the tin on a wire rack to cool completely, then remove from the tin and remove the paper. Put on a serving plate and decorate with gold leaf or icing sugar if you like. Serve.

Chocolate pavlova with salted caramel sauce

As indulgent desserts go, this has to be up there: crisp, chocolate meringue piled high with cream, bananas and a salted caramel sauce: heaven. The salted caramel sauce works brilliantly with anything chocolatey and, as you can imagine, it is just as happy drizzled over vanilla ice cream.

Serves 6–8

4 egg whites
225g (8oz) caster sugar
1½ tbsp cocoa powder
1 tsp cornflour
1 tsp red wine vinegar or
   balsamic vinegar
75g (2½oz) dark chocolate
   (55–62% cocoa solids),
   chopped, or chocolate
   drops, plus extra for
   grating
350ml (12fl oz) fresh double
   cream
3–4 bananas, to taste

For the salted caramel sauce

225g (8oz) caster or
   granulated sugar
100g (3½oz) butter
175ml (6fl oz) fresh double
   cream
salt

baking sheet

1. Preheat the oven to 150°C (300°F) Gas mark 2. Line the baking sheet with baking parchment. Put the egg whites in a clean, grease-free bowl and whisk with an electric beater until they form soft peaks, or use a food processor. Start adding the sugar while still whisking, 1 tablespoon at a time, until all the sugar is added and the mixture is thick, white and glossy.

2. Sift in the cocoa and the cornflour. Drizzle in the vinegar and scatter the chocolate over the top, then fold them all together lightly but thoroughly.

3. Turn out the meringue mixture on to the prepared baking sheet and use the back of a tablespoon to push the mixture into a circle about 20cm (8in) in diameter with a dip in the centre. The mixture will spread out a bit while baking, so make it thicker than you want it to be. Cook in the oven for 50 minutes, then turn off the oven and leave the pavlova to cool inside the oven.

4. To make the caramel sauce, put the sugar, butter and 75ml (2¼fl oz) water in a saucepan over a medium heat and stir while it heats up to dissolve the sugar and melt the butter.

5. Once the sugar has dissolved, turn the heat up to high and cook for 10 minutes until it turns a toffee colour. Do not stir the pan, although you might need to swirl it occasionally if you see it turning golden on one side of the pan before the other. Once the syrup is a rich golden toffee colour, stir in the cream and a good pinch of salt, then put the pan back over the heat for 2 minutes to dissolve the salt. Transfer to a jug. (It will store in the fridge for up to 3 months.)

6. When ready to serve, put the cream in a bowl and whip until soft peaks appear. Put the pavlova on a plate and top with the whipped cream. Slice the bananas at an angle and arrange over the cream. Drizzle with some salted caramel sauce and serve with more sauce and a grating of chocolate, if you wish.

Chocolate and hazelnut rum babas

You don't need to buy special baking tins to make these rum babas, although if you have them, do feel free to use them. Instead, I have used dariole moulds, which do the job just as well and are a lot more versatile to have in the kitchen. Hazelnuts and chocolate both go especially well with the caramel flavour of dark rum.

Serves 4

10g (¼oz) fresh yeast or
   1½ tsp active dried yeast
2 tbsp milk, lukewarm
140g (4¾oz) strong white
   bread flour, plus extra for
   dusting
salt
20g (¾oz) caster sugar
2 large eggs
40g (1½oz) melted butter,
   plus extra for greasing
12 tsp chopped toasted
   hazelnuts (see page 245)
50g (1¾oz) dark chocolate
   chips
whipped cream or vanilla
   ice cream, to serve

For the rum syrup

175g (6oz) caster sugar
4 tbsp dark rum

6 dariole moulds or baba
   tins

1. Put the yeast in a small bowl with the milk and stir together. Leave to stand for 5 minutes until creamy.

2. Sift the flour and a pinch of salt into a large mixing bowl and add the sugar. (You can use a stand mixer with a dough hook, if you prefer.) Add the eggs and the yeast mixture. Mix everything together, then add the butter and keep mixing for 5 minutes. The mixture will be quite runny. Cover the bowl and leave somewhere warm to rise for 40 minutes–1 hour, or until doubled in size.

3. Meanwhile, grease the dariole moulds generously with melted butter, paying particular attention to the bases, and dust with flour. Put 2 teaspoons of the chopped hazelnuts into the bottom of each mould.

4. Once the dough has risen, stir in the chocolate chips and spoon the mixture evenly into the moulds. Cover the moulds with cling film and leave to rise again for 15–20 minutes until the dough has risen almost to the top of the moulds. Preheat the oven to 190°C (375°F) Gas mark 5.

5. Bake for 15 minutes or until risen and golden on top. While cooking, make the syrup. Put the sugar in a saucepan over a medium-high heat and add 200ml (7fl oz) water. Heat, stirring, until all the sugar has dissolved, then cook until it reaches a rolling boil. Boil for 2 minutes, then add the rum, turn off the heat and set aside until the babas are ready.

6. While still in the moulds, skewer the tops of the babas a few times to make several holes in each, then pour over half the rum syrup and leave them to stand for 5 minutes.

7. Turn them out into shallow bowls and pour over the remaining syrup to soak the other side of the sponges. Serve with whipped cream or ice cream.

Galette des rois

A galette des rois, literally meaning 'kings' cake', is traditionally eaten in France to celebrate the Epiphany on 6 January, when the three kings arrived in Bethlehem. It is an impressive dessert made with puff pastry and filled with frangipane and cognac that is surprisingly easy to make once you have your puff pastry.

Serves 6

⅔ x quantity Puff Pastry (see page 238) or 750g (10oz) all-butter puff pastry
flour, for dusting
120g (4¼oz) ground almonds
50g (1¾oz) caster sugar
50g (1¾oz) icing sugar
2 tbsp cognac or dark rum
1 beaten egg

base of a 20cm (8in) and a 23cm (9in) cake tin (or plates of a similar size); two baking sheets

1. Roll out the pastry on a lightly floured work surface to 25 x 50cm (10 x 20in) and cut in half so you have two sqaures. Put one of the pastry squares on a lightly floured work surface and put the 20cm (8in) cake base on top. With a sharp knife, draw around the base to cut a clean circle. Move it to a baking sheet.

2. Repeat with the second pastry square, this time using the 23cm (9in) cake base or plate. Transfer to the other baking sheet. Chill both circles of pastry in the fridge for 1 hour. Meanwhile, put the ground almonds in a bowl and add the sugars and cognac. Mix together well to make a frangipane.

3. Spread the frangipane over the small pastry circle, leaving a 1cm (½in) border clear at the edge of the pastry. Brush the edge with the beaten egg.

4. Being very careful not to squash the filling and get it everywhere, put the large pastry circle on top and line up the edges with the circle below. Press together the edges to seal.

5. Knock up the pastry around the edges by placing two fingers on the edge and dragging the back of a knife between your fingers to create ridges around the tart. Brush the tart all over the top with the beaten egg, but don't let it drizzle down the sides or it might stick the puff pastry layers together and stop them rising.

6. Pierce a small hole in the centre of the tart using a skewer. Using a small, sharp knife, score curved lines in the pastry, going from the centre out to the edge so that it begins to resemble a Catherine wheel. Put it in the fridge to chill for 30 minutes. Preheat the oven to 200°C (400°F) Gas mark 6. Bake the galette for 45 minutes or until well risen and a dark golden brown. Serve warm or cold.

Blueberry and almond tart

This blueberry bakewell is made with the classic rich buttery pastry and soft frangipane filling. It's so simple to make, and yet it is always a crowd-pleaser.

Serves 8 – 10

1 x quantity Sweet
    Shortcrust Pastry (see
    page 235)
100g (3½oz) butter
100g (3½oz) caster sugar
1 egg, beaten and 1 egg yolk
100g (3½oz) ground
    almonds
25g (1oz) plain flour
2 tbsp kirsch (optional)
250g (9oz) blueberries
100ml (3½fl oz) apricot jam
softly whipped cream
    (optional), to serve

23cm (9in) flan ring and
    baking sheet or loose-
    bottomed tart tin with
    4cm (1½in) sides

1. Use the pastry to line the tin and bake blind as explained on page 236. Increase the oven temperature to 200°C (400°F) Gas mark 6.

2. Put the butter in a large bowl and cream it with a wooden spoon until soft, or use an electric beater on slow or a food processor. Add the sugar and beat until light and fluffy. Gradually add the egg and egg yolk, beating well after each addition.

3. Stir in the ground almonds and flour, then add the kirsch, if using. Pour this frangipane mixture into the pastry case and spread it evenly using the back of a spoon, then scatter the blueberries over the top.

4. Bake for 10 minutes, then reduce the oven temperature to 180°C (350°F) Gas mark 4 and continue cooking for 15–20 minutes until the frangipane is set in the centre and nicely golden. Meanwhile, put the jam in a small saucepan over a medium-low heat to dissolve gently, then push through a sieve into a small bowl.

5. Leave the tart to cool in the tin on a wire rack for 5 minutes, then brush the top generously with the apricot jam, to glaze the tart. Remove from the tin and transfer to a serving plate. Serve with whipped cream, if you like.

Baked crema Catalana

Crema Catalana is a Spanish version of the classic crème brûlée – a creamy custard with a crackly caramel crust. It often has flavourings such as orange, as here, and sometimes cinnamon added too. Traditionally, it is just made over the stove and set in the fridge, but by baking it you can get a deliciously smooth custard without the need for cornflour, which can make the texture less velvety.

Serves 6

1 vanilla pod
600ml (1 pint) fresh double
  cream
finely grated zest of 2
  oranges
6 egg yolks
125g (4½oz) caster sugar,
  plus extra for sprinkling

roasting tray; six 150ml
  (5fl oz) ramekins; chef's
  blowtorch

1. Preheat the oven to 150°C (300°F) Gas mark 2. Boil a kettleful of water. Split the vanilla pod lengthways and scrape out the seeds. Put the cream in a saucepan and add the vanilla seeds and pod and the orange zest. Heat gently to just below boiling point, then turn off the heat and leave the cream to infuse for 20 minutes.

2. Meanwhile, fold an old thick tea towel in half and put it in the bottom of the roasting tray. This will help to stop the ramekins overheating and overcooking the custard, and it will also make them less likely to slip when moving the tray to and from the oven. Put the ramekins in the tray and set aside.

3. Put the egg yolks in a mixing bowl and add the sugar, then whisk gently to combine (you don't want too much air in the mixture). Reheat the cream a little until it is hot but not boiling, then strain it into a bowl to remove the vanilla pod. Pour the cream on to the eggs and sugar, stirring constantly.

4. Pour the mixture into a jug and then pour evenly into the ramekins. Put the roasting tray on the centre shelf of the oven. Pour water from the kettle (it should have cooled a little by now) into the roasting tray to come halfway up the ramekins. Bake for 20–25 minutes until beginning to look set around the edges, but still having a wobble in the centre.

5. Remove from the oven and leave to cool in the tray. The residual heat will keep cooking the custards gently for a few minutes before they cool down. Remove from the roasting tray and chill the custards in the fridge until ready to serve.

6. Just before serving, sprinkle about 2 teaspoons sugar on to the top of each custard. Caramelise the sugar using a chef's blowtorch according to the manufacturer's instructions, until the sugar is dark brown and crisp, then serve within 30 minutes or the sugar will start to lose its crunch.

Strawberry and vanilla custard kataifi tart

I've travelled a bit around the Middle East and have been greatly inspired by the food culture there. Using kataifi pastry, which is made from shredded filo dough, is one of the favourite tips I picked up when travelling. Here, I have used them as a light, crispy base for this classic strawberry custard tart.

Serves 4

15g (½ oz) butter, softened
175g (6oz) kataifi pastry
50g (1¾oz) butter, melted
300g (11oz) caster sugar
250g (9oz) strawberries, hulled and cut into slices 5mm (¼in) thick (optional)
chopped pistachios, to serve

For the strawberry coulis

200g (7oz) strawberries, hulled
25–50g (1–1¾oz) caster sugar, to taste
juice of ½ lemon

For the custard

225g (8oz) caster sugar
2 eggs
90g (3¼oz) plain flour
500ml (18fl oz) milk
2–4 tsp rosewater, to taste
25g (1oz) butter, cubed

20cm (8in) springform cake tin

1. Preheat the oven to 180°C (350°F) Gas mark 4. To make the strawberry coulis, whizz the strawberries in a blender or food processor with a little of the sugar and the lemon juice. Add more sugar to taste, then push the mixture through a sieve into a jug. Store in the fridge until ready to serve.

2. Rub the 15g (½oz) softened butter over the base of the cake tin. Pull the kataifi pastry apart in a bowl and stir in the melted butter using your fingertips, then press the pastry into the base of the tin. Bake for 8–10 minutes until light golden.

3. While the pastry is cooking, put the sugar and 175ml (6fl oz) water in a saucepan over a medium-high heat and bring to the boil, stirring to dissolve the sugar. Boil for 1 minute.

4. When the pastry is cooked, pour the hot syrup (reheating it if necessary) over the pastry. Set aside and leave to cool.

5. To make the custard, put the sugar and the eggs in a bowl and whisk for 1 minute until fluffy, then whisk in the flour. Pour the milk into the saucepan over a medium-high heat. Bring to the boil, then pour the milk through a sieve on to the egg and flour mixture, whisking constantly.

6. Make sure the ingredients are thoroughly combined, then tip the mixture back into the saucepan and put over a low heat. Using a whisk, stir the mixture as it comes to the boil. It will thicken quickly when it boils, so whisk it to remove any lumps. Flavour with rosewater to taste, adding it gradually and continuing to whisk. Whisk in the butter, then take the pan off the heat. Pour the custard over the pastry, cover and leave to cool, then put in the fridge and leave to set.

7. When ready to serve, run a small, sharp knife around the sides of the tin to free the custard from the tin. Transfer to a serving plate, then arrange the sliced strawberries over the top of the tart in concentric circles. Serve with a drizzle of strawberry coulis over the tart and chopped pistachios.

Apple gratin

With its cinnamon and almond crumb topping, this delicious pudding is great to make when you have a surplus of apples to use up. Serve it with custard or lightly whipped cream.

Serves 6–8

butter, for greasing
700g (1lb 9oz) eating
  apples, peeled, cored and
  cut into 2cm (¾in) cubes
25g (1oz) sugar

For the gratin topping

75g (2½oz) butter, softened
100g (3½oz) caster sugar
2 eggs
100g (3½oz) ground
  almonds
½ tsp ground cinnamon
25g (1oz) flaked almonds

1 litre (1¾ pint) gratin or
  pie dish

1. Preheat the oven to 180°C (350°F) Gas mark 4. Butter the gratin dish. Put the apples in a saucepan and add the sugar and 2 tablespoons water. Cook the apples gently over a low heat, covered, for 5–7 minutes until half-cooked. Remove the lid and set aside.

2. To make the gratin topping, put the butter in a large bowl and cream it with a wooden spoon until soft, or use an electric beater on slow or a food processor. Add the sugar and beat until light and fluffy. Add the eggs one at a time, beating after each addition. Add the ground almonds and cinnamon, and mix until combined.

3. Spoon the apples and any liquid from the pan into the gratin dish, then spoon the gratin topping over the top, smoothing it out over the apples. Scatter the flaked almonds on top and bake for 20–25 minutes until firm to the touch and lightly golden on top.

Chocolate and coffee tart

Rich and indulgent, this is a sophisticated dessert for those who love their chocolate dark. You can grate the white chocolate over the top for ease, and you'll get little frothy curls reminiscent of a cappuccino. But if you're feeling like creating a real show-stopper, make your own white chocolate curls like those on the White Chocolate and Strawberry Celebration Cake on page 34.

Serves 8

1 x quantity Sweet
    Shortcrust Pastry (see
    page 235), substituting
    30g (1¼oz) of the flour
    with cocoa powder
150g (5½oz) butter
200g (7oz) dark chocolate
    (55–62% cocoa solids),
    roughly chopped
1½ tbsp powdered coffee
3 eggs and 3 egg yolks
40g (1½oz) sugar
cocoa powder, for dusting
50g (1¾oz) white
    chocolate, at warm room
    temperature

loose-bottomed 23cm (9in)
    tart tin

1. Line the tin with the pastry as explained in steps 1 and 2 on page 236 and prick the base with a fork. Put in the fridge to chill for 30 minutes. Preheat the oven to 190°C (375°F) Gas mark 5.

2. Line the pastry case with baking parchment and baking beans. Bake for 20 minutes, then remove the tin from the oven and check that the base of the pastry is dry. Remove the paper and beans, and return to the oven for another 3 minutes to dry it out completely.

3. Meanwhile, melt the butter and dark chocolate in a heatproof bowl over a pan of gently simmering water, making sure the base of the bowl doesn't touch the water, and stirring regularly. Remove the bowl from the heat and allow it to cool a little. Stir in the powdered coffee.

4. Put the eggs, yolks and sugar in a bowl and gently beat together, being careful not to get too much air into the mixture. Stir in the chocolate mixture, stirring until it's all combined.

5. Pour the mixture into the pastry case and return it to the oven. Bake for 6 minutes or until the outside is starting to look a little set, but there is still a distinct wobble in the centre. Allow the tart to cool in the tin.

6. Dust the top of the tart with cocoa powder. Using a fine grater, grate the white chocolate straight over the top of the tart so that the small curls fall directly on to the tart. Serve.

Tarte au citron

A subtle twist to the classic lemon-flavoured tarte au citron is to add lime, too, but it's one which isn't seen very frequently, unfortunately. Using both fruits really does lift the flavour of this tangy filling and makes it a much more exciting bite. The key with this tart is to cook it low and slow for the creamiest, smoothest custard centre. You could serve it with raspberries too, which love lime.

Serves 6 – 8

1 x quantity Sweet
　　Shortcrust Pastry (see
　　page 235)
4 large eggs
150g (5½oz) caster sugar
zest and juice of 1 large
　　juicy lemon
zest and juice of 3 large
　　juicy limes
140ml (4¾fl oz) fresh
　　double cream

23cm (9in) loose-bottomed
　　tart tin

1. Use the pastry to line the tin as explained in steps 1 and 2 on page 236, then prick over the base with a fork. Chill in the fridge for 30 minutes or the freezer for 10 minutes. Preheat the oven to 190°C (375°F) Gas mark 5.

2. Remove the pastry from the fridge and line it with baking parchment and baking beans. Cook for 20 minutes, then remove the tin from the oven and check that the bottom of the pastry is dry. Remove the paper and beans. If you have some beaten egg left over from making the pastry, you can brush some over the pastry before you return the tart to the oven for another 3 minutes to dry out completely. Remove the tart from the oven and lower the oven temperature to 150°C (300°F) Gas mark 2.

3. While the pastry is cooking, mix together the filling. Put the eggs and sugar in a bowl and blend together using an electric beater on a slow speed, or use a food processor – keep it gentle, as you don't want to add too much air to the mixture. Once blended, add the lemon and lime zest and juice, and the cream, and gently mix together.

4. Pour the mixture into the cooked case and return to the oven. Bake for 20 minutes or until the outside of the filling is starting to look a little set, but there is still a distinct wobble in the middle. Allow the tart to cool in the tin on a wire rack, then serve.

Strawberry and rose meringue

Meringues were one of my favourite things to bake when I was young, so I always like to include a recipe for one in my books. This one is such a simple summer classic: ripe, sweet strawberries, scented rose and whipped vanilla cream. You can prepare all the elements in advance – make the meringue, marinate the strawberries, crystallise the rose petals – but don't assemble it until the last minute or it will begin to go a bit soggy.

Serves 6

4 large egg whites
225g (8oz) caster sugar
1 tsp cornflour

For the crystallised rose petals

18 rose petals
1 egg white, lightly beaten
about 50g (1¾oz) caster
   sugar

For the topping

400g (14oz) small
   strawberries, hulled and
   cut in half
6 tbsp rosewater
½ vanilla pod
200ml (7fl oz) fresh double
   cream, whipped
20g (¾oz) icing sugar

two baking sheets

1. Line the baking sheets with baking parchment. Start by making the crystallised rose petals, as these will need a good few hours to dry. Gently brush each petal with egg white, then sprinkle with the sugar. Put on one of the prepared baking sheets and leave somewhere warm to dry out for a few hours until crisp. You can make these up to a day or two in advance, if you like.

2. Preheat the oven to 150°C (300°F) Gas mark 2. Draw 6 circles with a diameter of 10cm (4in) on the parchment on the unused baking sheet.

3. To make the meringue, put the egg whites in a clean, grease-free bowl and whisk with an electric beater until they form soft peaks, or use a food processor. Add a spoonful of the sugar and whisk until well combined. Continue in this way, adding a spoonful at a time and whisking in, until all the sugar has been added, then fold in the cornflour.

4. Spoon the mixture evenly into the circles you have drawn on the baking parchment and spread out to the edges, making sure the nests are a little higher around the edge than in the middle. Put in the oven, then immediately turn the oven temperature down to 120°C (250°F) Gas mark 1 and cook for 1 hour. Turn the oven off, but leave the meringues to cool in the oven until completely cold.

5. Meanwhile, prepare the topping. Put the strawberries in a bowl and drizzle over the rosewater, then toss to coat well. Leave to macerate for 2 hours to imbue the strawberries with a delicate rose flavour.

6. Split the vanilla pod lengthways and scrape out the seeds.
    Put the cream and vanilla seeds in a bowl and whisk until
    thickened, then gently stir in the icing sugar. You can do
    this a little in advance and store in the fridge, covered,
    overnight until needed.

7. To assemble, spoon the strawberries evenly into the dip in
    the centre of each meringue, drizzling any excess rosewater
    over as well, so that it seeps into the meringue and flavours
    it. Top the strawberries with a spoonful of the cream, then
    sprinkle the rose petals over the top and serve immediately.

Baked sweet saffron and condensed milk rice pudding

This is a wonderful end to a traditional Sunday lunch, and the perfect cosy and comforting treat when the weather turns cooler. Scented with saffron, with a creamy and almost caramel sweetness from the condensed milk, it is a delightfully old-fashioned pudding with a serious feel-good factor.

Serves 4

200g (7oz) pudding (pearl) rice
¼ tsp salt
900 ml whole milk
170ml (6fl oz) sweetened condensed milk
1 tsp vanilla extract
2 cinnamon sticks
a very small pinch of saffron threads
¼ teaspoon ground cinnamon, plus extra for dusting

3 litre (5¼ pint) ovenproof dish

1. Preheat the oven to 150°C (300°F) Gas mark 2. Put the rice into a 3 litre/5¼ pint ovenproof dish and add the salt, milk, condensed milk, vanilla extract, cinnamon sticks and saffron. Stir to combine, then bake for 2 hours. After 45 minutes remove it from the oven, give it a good stir and sprinkle over the cinnamon. Return to the oven and bake for the remaining hour and 15 minutes.

2. Discard the cinnamon sticks, give it a stir and ladle into bowls and if desired dust with a little extra cinnamon.

Baked caramel rice pudding

Wonderfully rich and creamy, this caramel rice pudding is divine served warm with chilled softly whipped cream and fresh berries. You can make the caramel sauce up to one day in advance and store it in the fridge in an airtight container. As it cools, it will thicken. To serve, gently reheat in a small saucepan until a drizzling consistency.

Serves 4 – 6

200g (7oz) Arborio rice
800ml (29fl oz) whole milk
50g (1¾oz) caster sugar
¼ tsp salt
1 vanilla pod
strawberries or raspberries
and softly whipped cream
(optional), to serve

For the caramel sauce

75g (2½oz) caster sugar
50g (1¾oz) unsalted butter,
diced
50ml (2fl oz) fresh double
cream

3 litre (5¼ pint) ovenproof
dish

1. Preheat the oven to 200°C (400°F) Gas mark 6. Put the rice into a 3 litre/5¼ pint ovenproof dish and add the milk, sugar and salt. Split the vanilla pod lengthways, scrape out the seeds and add to the dish with the empty pod. Stir to combine, cover with foil and bake for 1 hour.

2. In the meantime, make the caramel sauce. Put the sugar in a small saucepan and dissolve over a medium heat, swirling the pan occasionally to ensure that it dissolves evenly. Once the sugar has dissolved, increase the heat to medium-high and continue to cook until the sugar has turned a rich caramel colour. Remove the pan from the heat and add the butter and cream – be careful, as it will bubble. Put back on to the hob for another 1 minute or until fully combined, stirring occasionally. Pour the caramel sauce into a jug and set aside.

3. After the rice has cooked for 40 minutes, remove the foil and give it a good stir. Put it back in the oven, uncovered, for the remaining 20 minutes until the rice is completely cooked and creamy. Remove from the oven and let it rest for 5 minutes – it may seem like there is a lot of liquid remaining but this will continue to absorb as it stands. Discard the vanilla pods, gently stir together and ladle into bowls. Serve with chilled whipped cream and berries, if you like, and drizzle over the caramel sauce.

Tarte Tropézienne

This classic cake, as the name suggests, hails from St Tropez, and characterises that same effortless elegance that you would expect from there. A sweet, enriched brioche cake is sliced in half and simply filled with creamy vanilla crème pâtissière. The pearled sugar on top is optional, but I like to add it, as it's so pretty and luxurious, like jewels embedded in the cake, and is another wink to its namesake.

Serves 8

½ x quantity Classic Brioche dough (see page 241)
melted butter, for brushing
flour, for dusting
1 egg, beaten
pearled sugar nibs, to sprinkle
1 x quantity Crème Pâtissière (see page 242)

23cm (9in) loose-bottomed cake tin; piping bag with a plain nozzle

1. Make the brioche mix as explained in steps 1–3 on page 241. Cover the bowl with cling film or a plastic bag and put in the fridge to rest for 8–24 hours.

2. The following day, prepare the cake tin by brushing it with melted butter and dusting it with flour. Remove the dough from the fridge and knock it back in the bowl by folding it in on itself. It is crucial to work quickly at this stage, otherwise the butter will begin to melt and the dough will become too sticky to handle.

3. Form the dough into a neat round just smaller than the base of the tin. It's easiest to move the dough on to the base, then drop this into the sides of the tin. Brush the top of the loaf with the beaten egg.

4. Leave the brioche to rise in a warm place for 45 minutes– 1 hour until it has doubled in size. Preheat the oven to 180°C (350°F) Gas mark 4.

5. Gently brush the brioche with egg once more and sprinkle the top with pearled sugar nibs. Bake for 20 minutes. Cover with foil to stop it over-browning and bake for a further 10–15 minutes until risen and golden. It should sound almost hollow when tapped on the base after being removed from the tin. Leave on a wire rack to cool.

6. Once cool, slice the brioche in half horizontally and fill a piping bag with the crème pâtissière. Pipe or spread the crème pâtissière on to the bottom half of the brioche, then top with the top half and serve.

Baked fruit skewers

These are a smart choice if you want to make sure there's something just that bit healthier on the menu. It's also a good way to get little ones involved in cooking, as they will have great fun spearing fruit on to the skewers to make colourful, enticing desserts. Experiment with whichever fruit is in season, or stick to your favourites.

Serves 6

1 pineapple, peeled, cored
   and cut into 3cm (1¼in)
   pieces
4 nectarines, cut in half,
   stones removed and cut
   in half again
4 peaches, cut in half,
   stones removed and cut
   in half again
2 bananas, peeled and cut
   into 3cm (1¼in) pieces
½ tsp ground cinnamon
25g (1oz) caster sugar

To serve (optional)

1 tbsp honey
250ml (9fl oz) fresh double
   cream, lightly whipped

six 25cm (10in) skewers;
   baking sheet

1. If using wooden skewers, soak them for 30 minutes in cold water. Preheat the oven to 230°C (450°F) Gas mark 8. Line a baking sheet with baking parchment. Push the fruit on to the skewers and put on the prepared baking sheet.

2. Put the cinnamon and sugar in a small bowl and mix together. Using a teaspoon, sprinkle the sugar mixture over the fruit skewers. Bake for 10–14 minutes until the fruit is soft and nicely roasted.

3. The fruit will be very hot, so do be careful when you transfer the skewers from the baking sheet to a serving plate. If you like, stir the honey into the whipped cream and serve with the roasted fruit.

Breads

Cardamom and pistachio buns

There's nothing quite so appealing as this cluster of nutty buns, snuggled together and glistening with honey. They are ideal for sharing with a few friends around a pot of freshly brewed coffee.

Makes 12

50g (1¾oz) butter, softened, plus extra for greasing
375g (13oz) plain flour, plus extra for dusting
1 tsp baking powder
1 tsp ground cardamom
25g (1oz) caster sugar
1 egg
200ml (7fl oz) milk
2 tbsp runny honey
25g (1oz) pistachio nuts, shelled, lightly toasted (see page 245) and roughly chopped

For the filling

100g (3½oz) butter, softened
1 tsp ground cardamom
zest of 1 lemon
100g (3½oz) caster sugar
100g (3½oz) pistachio nuts, chopped

23cm (9in) cake tin with sides at least 4cm (1½in) high

1. Preheat the oven to 230°C (450°F) Gas mark 8. Grease the base and side of the cake tin, then dust lightly with flour. To make the filling, put the butter, cardamom and lemon zest in a large bowl and cream with a wooden spoon until soft, or use an electric beater on slow or a food processor. Add the sugar and beat until the mixture is light and fluffy. Stir in the nuts, then set aside at room temperature.

2. Sift the flour, baking powder and cardamom into a large bowl. Add the sugar and butter, then rub the butter into the dry ingredients using your fingertips until the mixture resembles breadcrumbs.

3. Whisk the egg and milk together in a separate bowl, then make a well in the centre of the dry ingredients and pour in most of the liquid, reserving about 60ml (2fl oz). Using one hand with your fingers outstretched like a claw, mix the dough by moving it around in one direction until it comes together. You might need to add the remaining milk, as the dough should be soft and a little sticky.

4. Tip the dough out on to a floured work surface and dust with flour. Using a rolling pin, roll out the dough to a 35 x 25cm (14 x 10in) rectangle. Spread the filling over the rectangle, then, with the widest end facing you, roll up the dough away from you so that it resembles a Swiss roll.

5. Cut the roll to make 12 slices, each 3cm (1¼in) thick. Put the pieces cut-side up in the prepared cake tin, leaving a tiny bit of space between each swirl. Bake for 10 minutes, then reduce the oven temperature to 200°C (400°F) Gas mark 6 and cook for a further 25–35 minutes until risen, golden brown and cooked in the centre. The buns should have joined together to make a lovely cluster.

6. Leave to rest in the tin for 3 minutes before carefully turning out on a wire rack to cool. While still warm, brush the honey over the top and decorate with the toasted pistachio nuts. To serve, break off each bun with your hand.

Baked doughnuts

These doughnuts work a treat in the oven, which is a great alternative if you aren't a fan of deep-frying. In this recipe, they are brushed with melted butter as they come out of the oven to give their classic sugar coating a little more sticking power.

Makes 10

115ml (3¾fl oz) milk,
  lukewarm
25g (1oz) caster sugar
10g (¼oz) fresh yeast or
  5g (⅛oz) active dried
  yeast
275g (10oz) strong
  white bread flour,
  plus extra for dusting
½ tsp salt
25g (1oz) butter, melted
1 egg, beaten
1 tsp vanilla extract

For the filling and topping

3 tbsp lemon curd (see
  page 104), or 3 tbsp
  raspberry jam, or
  3 tbsp Nutella
30g (1¼oz) caster sugar
30g (1¼oz) butter,
  melted

baking sheet; skewer;
  piping bag with a
  long piping tube

1. Pour the milk into a bowl and stir in the sugar, then add the yeast and leave to stand for 5 minutes until creamy.

2. Sift the flour and salt into the bowl of a food processor. Pour the melted butter into the yeast mixture followed by the egg and the vanilla extract, and stir well. Pour on to the flour and mix together using the paddle. Once combined, switch over to the dough hook and knead for 8–10 minutes until the mixture is coming away from the sides of the bowl. (Alternatively, mix the flour and melted butter mixture above using your hand until well incorporated. Turn the dough out on to a lightly floured work surface and knead the dough as explained on page 244.) The dough is ready when it is smooth and springy when you gently press it with a floured finger.

3. Cover the bowl with cling film (making sure there are no gaps for the air to get in) and put in a warm part of the kitchen for 1–2 hours or until doubled in size. It should be light and airy, and when you press the top of the dough with a floured finger, the dent from your finger should remain, and the dough should start to collapse.

4. Lightly flour the baking sheet. Take the dough out of the bowl and knead it by hand for 1 minute to knock all the air out. Divide the dough into 10 pieces. Take one piece and cover the rest with an upturned bowl to prevent a skin forming. Form the dough into a ball by rolling it on the work surface under the palm of your hand. Repeat with the other pieces. Don't flour the work surface too much, if at all, while you are rolling them or they won't grip and become smooth.

5. Once rolled, put them, smoother-side up and well spaced apart, on the prepared baking sheet, then flatten them with your hand until they look like burger buns, about 8cm (3¼in)

in diameter. Cover with a clean tea towel and put in a warm place for 20–30 minutes until light and slightly risen.

6. Preheat the oven to 180°C (350°F) Gas mark 4. When you press the dough gently with a floured finger, the dent of your finger should remain; the doughnuts are then ready for baking. Bake in the centre of the oven for 15 minutes or until golden brown; they should sound almost hollow when tapped on the base.

7. While the doughnuts are cooking, prepare the filling and topping. Put the lemon curd, jam or Nutella in a small saucepan over a low heat and gently warm through, stirring frequently. Put the sugar in a wide bowl.

8. When the doughnuts are cooked, brush them all over with the melted butter, then toss them in the sugar. Using a skewer, pierce each doughnut from the side into the centre and wiggle it around a little to make the hole larger, then pipe the lemon curd, jam or Nutella into the centre using the piping bag and long tube. Enjoy!

To make doughnut squares

Line a small 33 x 23cm (13 x 9in) Swiss roll tin with baking parchment. Roll out the dough after the first rising to fit into the tin. Lift into the prepared tin, then cover with a tea towel and put in a warm place for 30–40 minutes until doubled in size – when you press gently with a floured finger, the dent of your finger should remain; it is then ready for baking. Bake for 15–20 minutes until golden on top and light golden underneath. Brush very generously with 15g (½oz) melted butter and sprinkle with 25g (1oz) caster sugar, then leave for 10 minutes to cool slightly. Cut into squares to serve.

To make chocolate doughnut squares

Line a 33 x 23cm (13 x 9in) Swiss roll tin with baking parchment. Roll out half the dough after the first rising to fit into the tin. Lift into the prepared tin. Gently warm 175g (6oz) Nutella in a small saucepan over a low heat, then spread over the dough. Cover with the second half of dough. Leave to rise and bake, top with melted butter and sugar as for the doughnut squares above.

Cranberry and orange scones

Here is a delicious flavour twist on a classic scone to enjoy, sliced and thickly buttered. The scones also make good components for picnic hampers or lunchboxes. Although best on the day that they are baked, they are pretty quick to prepare and cook.

Makes 10–12

500g (1lb 2oz) plain flour, plus extra for dusting

1 rounded tsp bicarbonate of soda (bread soda)

2 rounded tsp cream of tartar

½ tsp salt

1 tsp ground mixed spice

125g (4½oz) cold butter, cubed

25g (1oz) caster sugar

100g (3½oz) dried cranberries

1 egg, beaten

275ml (9½fl oz) plus 1 tsp buttermilk

zest of 1 orange

baking sheet; 6cm (2½in) pastry cutter

1. Preheat the oven to 220°C (425°F) Gas mark 7. Dust the baking sheet with flour. Sift the flour, bicarbonate of soda, cream of tartar, salt and mixed spice into a large bowl. Using your fingertips, rub in the butter using your fingertips until the mixture resembles breadcrumbs. Add the sugar and cranberries, and mix well.

2. Set aside about one-third of the beaten egg and combine the remainder with the 275ml (9½fl oz) buttermilk and the orange zest in a bowl. Add to the flour mixture and mix to form a moist dough. Put on a lightly floured work surface and knead very slightly to bring the dough together. Press or roll it out to a thickness of 2cm (¾in).

3. Using the pastry cutter, cut out 12 scones and put them on the prepared baking sheet. Add the teaspoon of buttermilk to the remainder of the beaten egg to make an egg wash. Brush the scones with the egg wash and bake for 10–12 minutes until golden brown on top. Leave on a wire rack to cool completely.

Pistachio and cinnamon doughnuts

Lovely as doughnuts are, they are sometimes lacking in flavour and just a bit overwhelmingly sweet. It's not tricky to add a bit more interest by pepping up the sugar they are rolled in. Cinnamon and pistachio nuts make a great combination, but you could vary this with whichever spice and nuts are your favourites.

Makes about 20

350ml (12fl oz) lukewarm
   water
2 tbsp honey
20g (¾oz) fresh yeast or 10g
   (¼oz) active dried yeast
300g (11oz) plain flour
25g (1oz) cornflour
1 tsp ground cinnamon
½ tsp salt
sunflower oil, for deep-
   frying

For the coating

75g (2½oz) pistachio nuts,
   chopped
2 tbsp granulated sugar
½ tsp ground cinnamon

1. Pour the lukewarm water into a bowl or jug and stir in the honey. Add the yeast and leave to stand for 5 minutes or until creamy. Sift the flour, cornflour, cinnamon and salt into a bowl, and mix well.

2. Pour the yeast mixture into the dry ingredients and stir well to mix. Cover with cling film and leave to stand at room temperature for 30 minutes or until bubbles start to appear on the surface. (The doughnut batter can also be put in the fridge, where it will rest perfectly for up to 24 hours.)

3. To make the coating, put the chopped nuts in a wide bowl and add the sugar and cinnamon. Mix together.

4. Heat the oil in a deep-fryer to 180°C (350°F), or use a large saucepan over a medium-high heat (test by frying a small cube of bread; it should brown in 40 seconds).

5. Using a dessertspoon, scoop out a spoonful of the batter and use another dessertspoon to scrape it into the oil. Add a few more spoonfuls of batter to the oil, but don't overcrowd the pan or the temperature will drop, resulting in oily and heavy doughnuts. I like to cook about 6 at a time.

6. Allow the doughnuts to cook for 2 minutes or until golden underneath, then turn them over using a slotted spoon and cook on the other side for 2 minutes or until golden and cooked through in the centre.

7. Using the slotted spoon, lift the doughnuts out of the oil and into the cinnamon and pistachio sugar. Toss well so that the nut sugar sticks to the still oily doughnuts. Serve straight away.

Kouign-amann

Think of a layered, rich, buttery croissant, with plenty of extra sugar and a hint of sea salt, and that is where this wonderful recipe will take you. It comes from Brittany in northern France and its translation from the Breton language literally means 'butter cake'. The salt only serves to bring out the buttery flavour even more, and the sugar caramelises in the tin, so you have to remove them quickly after they are baked so that they don't stick fast!

Makes 12

20g (¾ oz) fresh yeast or 10g (¼oz) active dried yeast

200ml (7fl oz) lukewarm water

280g strong white bread flour, plus extra for dusting

120g (4¼oz) caster sugar, plus extra for sprinkling and for the tins

½ tsp salt

150g (5½oz) butter, chilled, plus extra for greasing

2 tsp sea salt flakes

12-hole muffin tray

1. Put the yeast in a small bowl with 2 tablespoons of the warm water and stir to dissolve, then leave to stand for 5 minutes until creamy.

2. Sift the flour, 20g (¾oz) of the sugar and the salt into a large bowl. (You can use a stand mixer with a dough hook, if you prefer.) Pour in the yeast mixture and mix well, gradually adding the remaining water.

3. If kneading by hand, turn out on to a lightly floured work surface and knead strongly (see page 244) for 8–10 minutes. It should be springy when you press the dough with your finger. (If using a stand mixer, kneading will take about 5 minutes.)

4. Rub some butter around the inside of the bowl, then put the dough in the bowl, cover with cling film and leave to rise in a warm part of your kitchen for 1 hour or until the dough has doubled in size.

5. Put the dough on a lightly floured work surface and roll it out to a 25cm (10in) circle. Take the butter from the fridge and put it between 2 sheets of greaseproof paper. Using a rolling pin, pound the butter to spread it out to a 10 x 15cm (4 x 6in) rectangle.

6. Put the butter in the middle of the dough circle and fold the right-hand side of the circle over the butter. Lift the left-hand side over, overlapping the dough in the centre. Now fold the top of the dough circle down over the butter, followed by folding the bottom of the dough circle up to just overlap with the previous fold.

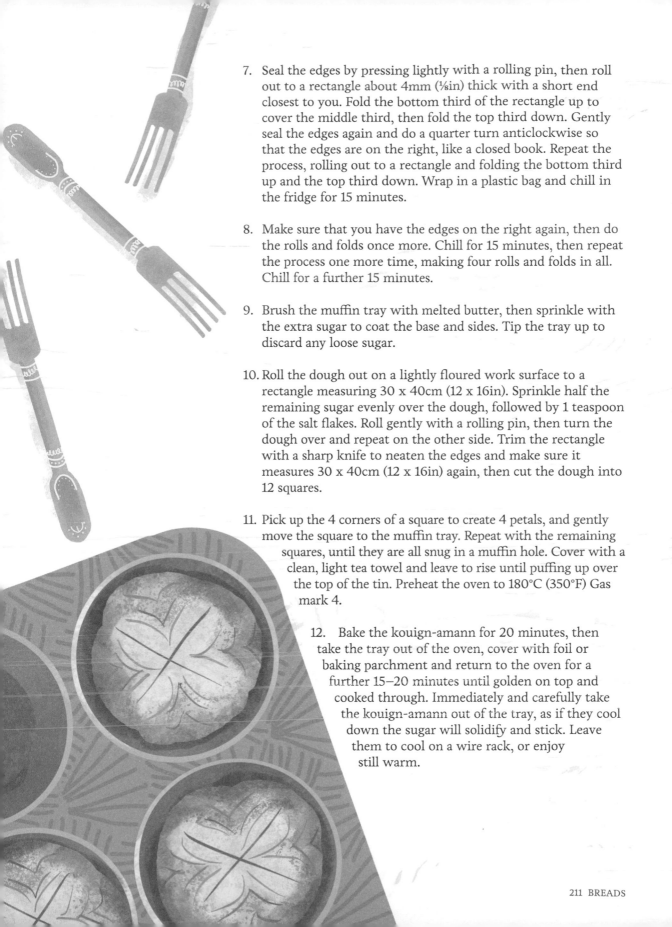

7. Seal the edges by pressing lightly with a rolling pin, then roll out to a rectangle about 4mm (⅛in) thick with a short end closest to you. Fold the bottom third of the rectangle up to cover the middle third, then fold the top third down. Gently seal the edges again and do a quarter turn anticlockwise so that the edges are on the right, like a closed book. Repeat the process, rolling out to a rectangle and folding the bottom third up and the top third down. Wrap in a plastic bag and chill in the fridge for 15 minutes.

8. Make sure that you have the edges on the right again, then do the rolls and folds once more. Chill for 15 minutes, then repeat the process one more time, making four rolls and folds in all. Chill for a further 15 minutes.

9. Brush the muffin tray with melted butter, then sprinkle with the extra sugar to coat the base and sides. Tip the tray up to discard any loose sugar.

10. Roll the dough out on a lightly floured work surface to a rectangle measuring 30 x 40cm (12 x 16in). Sprinkle half the remaining sugar evenly over the dough, followed by 1 teaspoon of the salt flakes. Roll gently with a rolling pin, then turn the dough over and repeat on the other side. Trim the rectangle with a sharp knife to neaten the edges and make sure it measures 30 x 40cm (12 x 16in) again, then cut the dough into 12 squares.

11. Pick up the 4 corners of a square to create 4 petals, and gently move the square to the muffin tray. Repeat with the remaining squares, until they are all snug in a muffin hole. Cover with a clean, light tea towel and leave to rise until puffing up over the top of the tin. Preheat the oven to 180°C (350°F) Gas mark 4.

12. Bake the kouign-amann for 20 minutes, then take the tray out of the oven, cover with foil or baking parchment and return to the oven for a further 15–20 minutes until golden on top and cooked through. Immediately and carefully take the kouign-amann out of the tray, as if they cool down the sugar will solidify and stick. Leave them to cool on a wire rack, or enjoy still warm.

Chocolate brioche swirl loaf

I love seeing our students' thrilled faces at the cookery school when they've taken their first batch of brioche out of the oven. This divinely rich, yet light, bread is much easier to make than you'd imagine. It's well worth using a stand mixer to knead the dough to prevent the butter melting with the heat of your hands.

Serves 4–6

⅓ x quantity of Classic Brioche dough (see page 241)
flour, for dusting
150g (5½oz) dark chocolate (55–62% cocoa solids), chopped, or chocolate drops
1 egg, beaten
icing sugar, for dusting

900g (2lb) loaf tin

1. Line the loaf tin with baking parchment. Roll out the dough on a lightly floured work surface to 20 x 30cm (8 x 12in). Scatter over the chocolate and press it into the dough. Roll up from the short end and put into the prepared loaf tin.

2. Cover with a clean tea towel and leave to rise in a warm place in the kitchen (warm room temperature is ideal) for 1 hour or until light and risen.

3. Preheat the oven to 180°C (350°F) Gas mark 4. Brush the top of the loaf gently with beaten egg and bake for 25–30 minutes until deep golden on top and golden underneath. The brioche should sound almost hollow when tapped on the base. Turn out of the tin and leave on a wire rack to cool slightly. Dust with icing sugar, cut into slices and serve.

Croissants

Every baking book needs a recipe for a classic croissant, so here it is. Roll and fold to your heart's delight! But if you do just want to pop to the bakery around the corner, I won't judge you.

Makes 12

20g (¾oz) fresh yeast or 10g (¼oz) active dried yeast
300ml (11fl oz) lukewarm water
30g (1¼oz) caster sugar
450g (1lb) strong white bread flour, plus extra for dusting
½ tsp salt
200g (7oz) butter, chilled
1 large egg, beaten

two baking sheets

1. Put the yeast in a small bowl with 2 tablespoons of the warm water and the sugar. Stir together, then leave to stand for 5 minutes until creamy.

2. Sift the flour and salt into a large bowl. (You can use a stand mixer with a dough hook, if you prefer.) Tip the yeast mixture into the flour and mix, gradually adding the remaining water, until you have a soft dough. Turn out on to a lightly floured work surface and knead strongly (see page 244) for 10 minutes. It should be springy when you press the dough with your finger. (If using a stand mixer and a dough hook, kneading will take about 5 minutes.)

3. Put the dough in a bowl, cover with cling film and leave to rise in a warm place for 1 hour, or until doubled in size.

4. Roll out the dough on a lightly floured work surface to a 35cm (14in) circle. Take the butter out of the fridge and put it between 2 sheets of baking parchment. Using a rolling pin, pound the butter to spread it out to a rectangle about 5mm (¼in) thick. Put the butter in the middle of the dough circle and fold the right-hand side of the circle over the butter. Lift the left-hand side over, overlapping the dough in the middle. Now fold the top of the dough circle down over the butter, followed by folding the bottom of the dough circle up to just overlap with the previous fold.

5. Seal the edges by pressing lightly with a rolling pin, then roll out to a rectangle about 4mm (⅛ in) thick with a short end closest to you, starting with 'rib rolling' (see step 4 page 239). Fold the bottom third of the rectangle up to cover the middle third, then fold the top third down. Gently seal the edges again and do a quarter turn anticlockwise so that the edges are on the right, like a closed book.

6. Repeat the process, rolling out to a rectangle and folding the bottom third up and the top third down. Wrap in a plastic bag and chill in the fridge for 15 minutes.

7. Make sure you have the edges on the right again, then roll and fold again. Chill for 15 minutes, then repeat the process one more time, making four rolls and folds in all. Chill for a further 15 minutes. Line the baking sheets with baking parchment.

8. The next part is easiest if you work with half the dough at a time, so slice the dough in half widthways. Keeping one piece covered with cling film so that it doesn't dry out, roll out the other piece to a 56 x 20cm (22 x 8in) rectangle. Cut the dough into triangles 18cm (7in) at the base and 20cm (8in) sides – you should get 6 from this piece, although you may need to form the final one with the offcuts from both ends.

9. Cut a nick in the dough halfway along the base (this will help them roll more easily) and roll them up from the base towards the tip. Transfer the croissants to the prepared baking sheet, curling the ends towards you into a crescent as you put them down, and cover with a clean, light tea towel. Repeat with the other piece of dough, put those on the second baking sheet and cover.

10. Leave the croissants to rise in a warm part of the kitchen, but don't let them get too hot or the butter will melt and affect how they rise. Preheat the oven to 220°C (425°F) Gas mark 7.

11. Brush the croissants with beaten egg and bake for 13–15 minutes, until well risen and golden. Leave on a wire rack to cool or eat warm.

Pain aux raisins

Here is the classic pain aux raisins recipe, but there's no reason why you can't take it and mix things up a bit, if you're feeling adventurous. Try switching the raisins for chocolate drops, dried cranberries or cherries, or roasted hazelnuts – the list is endless.

Makes 12

175g (6oz) butter, chilled and cut into small dice
25g (1oz) plain flour
15g (½oz) fresh yeast or 7g (¼oz) active dried yeast
80ml (2½fl oz) whole milk, lukewarm
225g (8oz) strong white bread flour, plus extra for dusting
20g (¾oz) caster sugar
1 egg, beaten

For the filling and topping

½ x quantity Crème Pâtissière (see page 242)
75g (2½oz) raisins
1 egg, beaten
150g (5½oz) icing sugar

two baking sheets; pastry cutter (optional)

1. Put the butter and plain flour in a mixing bowl. Rub the butter into the flour using your fingertips until well combined (a pastry cutter is very useful for this, especially if you have hot hands). Form the mixture into a rectangle, wrap it in cling film and chill it in the fridge for at least 45 minutes or until it hardens. (You can do this well in advance and leave it in the fridge until you need it.)

2. Put the yeast in a small bowl and blend it with a little of the warm milk. Leave to stand for 5 minutes until creamy. Sift the bread flour into a large bowl and add the sugar. (You can use a stand mixer with a dough hook, if you prefer.)

3. Make a well in the centre of the flour mixture and pour in the yeast mixture and egg. Mix, gradually trickling in the remaining milk, until you have a smooth, soft dough.

4. If kneading by hand, turn out on to a lightly floured work surface and knead strongly (see page 244) for 8–10 minutes. It should be springy when you press the dough with your floured finger. (If using a stand mixer, kneading will take about 5 minutes.)

5. Roll out the dough on a lightly floured work surface, to roughly 35cm (14in) square. Take the butter dough from the fridge and put it between two pieces of baking parchment. Using a rolling pin, tap it firmly to flatten it and spread it out to a 15 x 30cm (6 x 12in) rectangle. Put it on the right-hand side of the bread-dough square and fold the left side of the bread dough over the butter dough to completely enclose it. The bread dough should meet at the right-hand edge, so press here gently with your rolling pin to seal the join.

6. Roll out the dough until it is about 5mm (¼in) thick. Gently mark the dough into thirds and fold the bottom third up into the middle, then fold the top third down over that. Seal the edges again and give the rectangle a quarter turn anticlockwise, so that the edges are now on the right, like a closed book.

7. Roll out again, folding the bottom third up and the top third down, then seal the edges. Put in a plastic bag and chill for 30 minutes.

8. Repeat the rolling and folding process twice more, making sure you start where you left off, with the edges on the right. Chill again for 30 minutes–2 hours until required.

9. Line the baking sheets with baking parchment. Take the dough from the fridge and roll it out to a 35cm (14in) square about 3mm (⅛in) thick on a lightly floured work surface. Spread the crème pâtissière all over the dough and scatter the raisins evenly over the top.

10. Roll the square up into a sausage and cut it into 12 even slices using a sharp knife. Lay the spiral slices on the prepared baking sheets, cut side up, and cover lightly with cling film. Leave to rise again in a warm place. Preheat the oven to 220°C (425°F) Gas mark 7. Brush the spirals all over with the beaten egg and bake for 12–15 minutes, until golden brown.

11. Sift the icing sugar into a bowl and mix with about 1 tablespoon water to make an icing that you can drizzle, then drizzle it all over the pastries on the tray. Eat warm or leave to cool and enjoy.

Southern cornbread

A big, hearty pan of chilli con carne needs a golden chunk of cornbread to go with it, and this is a recipe I adore. Some cornbreads are just simple breads, substituting cornmeal for wheat flour, but this one has a character all of its own: chilli, sweetcorn, spring onions, cheese and coriander all give it a wonderful flavour.

Serves 8 – 10

125g (4½oz) butter, melted, plus extra for greasing
2 eggs
450ml buttermilk
½ tsp Tabasco sauce
6 spring onions, finely sliced
2 tbsp chopped fresh coriander leaves
1 mild red chilli, deseeded and finely chopped
125g (4½oz) sweetcorn, tinned or frozen, thawed
40g (1½oz) Cheddar cheese, grated
190g (6¾oz) medium cornmeal (also called medium polenta or medium maizemeal)
50g (1¾oz) caster sugar
1½ tsp salt
175g (6oz) plain flour
1½ tsp baking powder
¼ tsp bicarbonate of soda (bread soda)
butter, to serve

20cm (8in) square cake tin with high sides

1. Preheat the oven to 220°C (425°F) Gas mark 7. Grease and line the base and sides of the tin with baking parchment. Pour the butter into a large bowl and add the eggs. Whisk well, then stir in the buttermilk, Tabasco sauce, spring onions, coriander, chilli, sweetcorn and grated cheese.

2. Put the cornmeal in a large mixing bowl and add the sugar and salt, then stir to mix. Sift in the flour, baking powder and bicarbonate of soda, then mix well. Make a well in the centre and add the wet ingredients, then mix well to combine.

3. Pour the batter into the prepared tin and bake on one of the lower shelves of the oven for 40 minutes or until golden brown and a skewer inserted into the centre comes out clean. Cut into squares and enjoy with butter, if you like.

Jewelled kanellängd

Having an Icelandic mother, I have grown up with a fondness for Scandinavian flavours such as cardamom, and the wonderfully plaited breads those spices so often perfume. Throw in some figs and crystallised ginger, and you have a bread that not only looks amazing but has plenty of interest for your taste buds, too.

Serves 10–12

40g (1½oz) butter, melted, plus extra for greasing
15g (½oz) fresh yeast or 7g (¼oz) active dried yeast
225ml (8fl oz) milk, lukewarm
400g (14oz) strong white bread flour, plus extra for dusting
30g (1¼oz) caster sugar
½ tsp salt
1 egg yolk, plus 1 beaten egg
zest of 1 orange

For the filling and topping

75g (2½oz) butter, softened
75g (2½oz) soft dark brown sugar
1 tsp ground cardamom
40g (1½oz) crystallised ginger, cut into small pieces
60g (2¼oz) firm dried figs, cut into small pieces
75g (2½oz) icing sugar
30g (1¼oz) undyed glacé cherries, or dried cranberries or cherries, chopped

baking sheet

1. Line the baking sheet with baking parchment and lightly grease a mixing bowl. Put the yeast in a small bowl and cover with a little of the warm milk. Stir together, then leave to stand for 5 minutes until creamy.

2. Put the flour, sugar and salt in a large bowl. (You can use a stand mixer with a dough hook, if you prefer.) Add the yeast mixture, melted butter, egg yolk, orange zest and half the remaining milk. Mix to a dough, gradually adding the remaining milk (you may not need it all) until you have a soft dough.

3. If kneading by hand, turn out on to a lightly floured work surface and knead strongly (see page 244) for 8–10 minutes. It should be springy when you press the dough with your floured finger. (If using a stand mixer, kneading will take about 5 minutes.)

4. Put it in the greased bowl, cover with cling film and leave to rise in a warm part of your kitchen for 1 hour or until doubled in size.

5. Meanwhile, to make the filling, put the butter in a bowl and add the sugar and cardamom. Combine well.

6. Roll out the dough on a lightly floured work surface to a 35cm (14in) square. Spread thinly with the butter mixture, then sprinkle most of the ginger and figs over the square, reserving a little of each to decorate.

7. Roll up the pastry carefully and move the roll to the prepared baking sheet. Using large, sharp scissors, snip along the length of the dough to make deep cuts without cutting through to the base of the loaf – the slices must still be attached underneath.

8. Carefully rearrange the slices, pulling one to the right and then the next to the left, and so on, along the length of the dough. Loosely cover with a clean, light tea towel and leave to rise for another 30 minutes, until the dough no longer springs back when gently prodded. Preheat the oven to 200°C (400°F) Gas mark 6.

9. Brush the dough all over with beaten egg, then bake for 25–30 minutes or until golden, risen and cooked through. Leave to cool on the baking sheet on a wire rack.

10. Make the icing by mixing the icing sugar with 1 tablespoon water to make an icing that you can drizzle. Drizzle it over the loaf, then sprinkle with the remaining ginger and figs, and the cherries and cranberries.

Naan breads

Naan breads would traditionally be cooked on the inside of the tandoor oven: stuck to the wall, where they would cook on one side from the heat of the metal and on the other from the hot air of the oven. You can go some way to replicating this by heating a very heavy baking sheet and transferring the thinly rolled dough to that, which will make the breads cook in a very short time. Brush them generously with melted butter straight from the oven.

Makes 6

20g (¾oz) fresh yeast or 10g (¼oz) active dried yeast
200ml (7fl oz) whole milk, lukewarm
500g (1lb 2oz) strong white bread flour
1 tsp salt
2 tsp sugar
1 egg, beaten
125g (4½oz) plain yoghurt
1 tbsp sunflower oil, plus extra for greasing

For the coriander and garlic flavouring

60g (2¼oz) butter, melted
2 garlic cloves, crushed
20g (¾oz) fresh coriander leaves, chopped
sea salt flakes, for sprinkling

two heavy baking sheets

1. Put the yeast in a small bowl and add a little of the warm milk. Stir together, then leave to stand for 5 minutes until creamy.

2. Sift the flour and salt into a large bowl and add the sugar. (You can use a stand mixer with a dough hook, if you prefer.) Make a well in the centre and add the yeast mixture, egg, yoghurt, oil and the remaining milk. Mix to a soft dough.

3. If kneading by hand, turn out on to a lightly floured work surface and knead strongly (see page 244), for 10–15 minutes. It should be springy when you press the dough with your finger. (If using a stand mixer, use a dough hook and kneading will take about 10 minutes.) You should have a soft, smooth dough.

4. Grease the mixing bowl with a little oil and transfer the dough to the bowl, turning it in the oil to coat. Cover with cling film and leave to rise in a warm part of the kitchen for about 1 hour or until doubled in size. Preheat the oven to 220°C (425°F) Gas mark 7 and turn on the grill to its highest setting. Put the baking sheets in the oven to heat up well.

5. Put the melted butter and garlic for the flavouring in a small bowl. Mix well and set aside. Roll out the dough on a floured work surface. Sprinkle the coriander over half the dough and fold the other half over so that the coriander is sandwiched. Roll out again and fold to fully seal the herbs within the dough. Cut the dough into 6 pieces and cover them with cling film.

6. Roll out a piece of dough to about 3mm (⅛in) thick in a teardrop shape. Carefully, but quickly, take one of the hot trays from the oven and transfer the dough to it. Put it back in the oven for 5 minutes or until the bread puffs up. Depending on your oven, it might be browned on top; if not, pop it under the grill for a few seconds to brown the top. Remove from the oven or grill and wrap the bread in a clean tea towel to keep warm while you make the others.

7. Repeat the process with the other 5 pieces of dough, alternating baking sheets as you go so that one is always warming up again. Put the cooked naans stacked together in the clean tea towel to keep them warm and soft. Brush them with the garlic butter and sprinkle generously with sea salt flakes, then serve.

Variation: For spice seed naan, combine 1½ teaspoons nigella seeds, 1½ teaspoons black mustard seeds and ¼ teaspoon cumin seeds in a small bowl. Roll the plain dough (without the coriander and garlic flavouring) into a teardrop shape as above and sprinkle it with about ½ teaspoon of the spice seed mix and a generous pinch of sea salt flakes. Roll gently over the top with the rolling pin to press the spices into the dough. Cook as above. Melt 60g (2¼oz) butter, and use to brush over the bread when it is cooked.

Pita breads

An essential in my busy family kitchen, pita breads are always on hand and are happy to be packed with whatever treasures might be found in the fridge: cheese, ham, salad, pickles – you name it. They also freeze well.

Makes 8–10

325ml (11½fl oz) lukewarm
    water
1 tsp sugar
25g (1oz) fresh yeast or 12g
    (½oz) active dried yeast
450g (1lb) strong white
    bread flour, plus extra for
    dusting
1 tsp salt
olive oil, for greasing

two baking sheets

1. Pour the lukewarm water into a measuring jug and stir in the sugar. Crumble in the yeast and leave to stand for 5 minutes or until creamy. Sift the flour and salt into a large bowl. You can use a stand mixer with a dough hook, if you prefer. Pour in the yeast mixture and mix well.

2. If kneading by hand, turn out on to a lightly floured work surface and knead strongly (see page 244) for 8–10 minutes. It should be springy when you press the dough with your finger. (If using a stand mixer, kneading will take about 5 minutes.)

3. Rub some olive oil around the inside of the bowl and turn the dough so that the whole surface is oiled. Cover with cling film and leave to rise in a warm part of your kitchen for 1–2 hours or until the dough has more than doubled in size. The dough should be very light and have some bubbles appearing on the surface. When you gently press it with a floured finger the dough should start to collapse.

4. Take the dough out of the bowl and knead it by hand for 1 minute to knock all the air out. Roll the dough into a thick log and divide it into 8–10 equal-sized pieces. Take one piece and cover the remaining pieces with an upturned bowl to prevent a skin forming. Form the dough into a ball by rolling it on the work surface under the palm of your hand. Put on to a floured work surface, then cover. Repeat with the remaining pieces of dough and leave to rise for 30 minutes or until doubled in size again.

5. Preheat the oven to 230°C (450°F) Gas mark 8 and put the baking sheets in the oven to heat up. Roll out the dough balls to make circles about 15cm (6in) in diameter and 5mm (¼in) thick, and dust both sides with flour. Cover with clean tea towels and leave to stand for 5 minutes.

6. Put 2 or 3 pita breads at a time on to a hot baking sheet and bake for 3 minutes or until very light golden brown and puffed. If not using immediately, leave the pita breads to cool on wire racks covered with a tea towel.

Variation: For sesame pita breads, roll each ball of dough in 1 teaspoon black or white sesame seeds before rolling it into a circle.

Easy soda red onion, olive and rosemary focaccia

This simple focaccia, full of Provençal flavours, is a great accompaniment to summer salads or autumnal soups. It is a blend of an Irish soda bread and an Italian focaccia and uses bicarbonate of soda (bread soda) for a quick but still delicious result. Eat while fresh and warm – it can be popped back into the oven to reheat after baking.

Serves 10 – 12

a good drizzle of extra virgin olive oil, about 50–75ml (2–3fl oz), plus extra for greasing

450g (1lb) plain flour, plus extra for dusting

1 tsp salt

½ tsp bicarbonate of soda (bread soda)

400ml (14fl oz) buttermilk, or sour milk (for dairy-free, see tip)

1 red onion, cut into 8 wedges

12 pitted black or green olives

a few sprigs of rosemary, broken into 12 little pieces

sea salt flakes, to sprinkle

33 x 23cm (13 x 9in) Swiss roll tin

1. Preheat the oven to 230°C (450°F) Gas mark 8. Brush the inside of the Swiss roll tin generously with olive oil. Sift the flour, salt and bicarbonate of soda into a large bowl, then make a well in the centre. Pour all but 2 tablespoons of the buttermilk in at once. Using one hand, shaped like a claw, mix in the flour from the sides of the bowl, adding more buttermilk if necessary. The dough should be soft and sticky.

2. When it all comes together, turn it out on to a floured work surface and turn it over in the flour once, but make sure not to knead it in any way or you will make it tough. Gently roll it out so that it will fit into the tin. Transfer to the prepared tin using both your hands.

3. Make dimples in the dough using the tips of your fingers, to make little wells for the olive oil. Scatter the onion wedges, the olives and the rosemary sprigs over the dough, pressing them all down gently so that they don't fall off the bread when it is baked. Drizzle generously with olive oil, and sprinkle with sea salt.

4. Bake for 25–30 minutes. The bread should be golden on the top and underneath. If the bread is a good golden colour but is not fully cooked, reduce the oven temperature to 200°C (400°F) Gas mark 6 and continue cooking for another 5 minutes.

5. Drizzle a little more olive oil over the top of the cooked, hot loaf. Turn out and leave to cool slightly on a wire rack before serving.

Tip: You can use a plant-based milk such as almond milk or rice milk, but add 1 tablespoon vinegar (such as white wine vinegar) and leave it to stand for 2 minutes before using.

Cumin and coriander flatbreads

This flatbread is a delicious vehicle for scooping up or dipping into all my favourite mezze-type dishes, such as hummus, tabbouleh, tzatziki or even guacamole. Feel free to try other things in the dough apart from cumin and coriander, such as chopped spring onion and rosemary, or a small squeeze of tomato purée and some torn basil leaves. The flatbreads are really good warm (but also good cold) and you can reheat them wrapped in foil in the oven, heated to 180°C (350°F) Gas mark 4.

Makes 6 breads

225g (8oz) plain flour, plus extra for dusting
2 tsp baking powder
¾ tsp salt
1 generous tsp cumin seeds, freshly ground
3 tbsp chopped fresh coriander leaves
3 tbsp sunflower oil, plus extra for frying
150–200ml (5–7fl oz) boiling water
sea salt, to serve

1. Sift the flour, baking powder, salt and cumin into a large bowl and add the coriander. In a separate bowl, mix the oil and 150ml (5fl oz) of the boiling water and add it to the dry ingredients. Stir to combine to a soft dough – you may need more water.

2. Knead with your hands on the work surface for 2 minutes, using extra flour if the dough sticks to the surface. Wrap the dough in a plastic bag or cling film and leave to rest for at least 15 minutes.

3. Divide the dough into 6 equal pieces and roll each portion on a lightly floured work surface to a 20cm (8in) circle. Heat a frying pan over a medium heat and add 2 tablespoons oil. Add 1 bread round, cover the pan with a lid or plate, and reduce the heat to low. Cook for 3 minutes or until golden brown underneath, then flip it over and cook the other side.

4. When the bread is golden on both sides, remove it from the pan and drain on kitchen paper, then wrap in a clean tea towel to keep it soft. Repeat with the remaining rounds of dough, wrapping them in the tea towel, stacked together. Serve whole, or cut each round into wedges and sprinkle with sea salt.

Multi-seed brown bread

This is a recipe from Anne Zagar, a chef in my restaurant and my friend. It has travelled through all the places she has worked in and the bread always comes out the same, making it her go-to loaf for all occasions. The bread will be delicious for a couple of days and will toast perfectly for days after. Keep it wrapped or freeze it for another day and it will become a staple in your kitchen too. If you can resist cutting it too early, it's best to leave it to cool for 20 minutes and then tuck in!

Makes 1 loaf

oil, for greasing
60g (2¼oz) mixed seeds,
    such as sesame, linseed,
    sunflower and pumpkin,
    plus extra for sprinkling
280g (10oz) coarse plain
    wholemeal flour
160g (5¾oz) self-raising
    flour
20g (¾oz) baking powder
1 tsp salt
90–100g (3¼–3½oz) golden
    syrup, as needed
300ml (11fl oz) buttermilk
120–150ml (4½–5fl oz)
    milk, as needed

900g (2lb) loaf tin

1. Preheat the oven to 170°C (325°F) Gas mark 3. Grease the loaf tin and scatter a few seeds over the base. Put the flours, baking powder and salt in a bowl, then add the seeds and stir well to combine. (You can use a food processor with a paddle, if you prefer.)

2. If making by hand, put the golden syrup in a small saucepan over a medium heat to melt it – this will make it easier to mix without causing the ingredients to clump together. It is not necessary to heat it if you are using a food processor.

3. Gradually add the golden syrup to the bowl, mixing well, so that it starts to colour the flour mixture without causing it to clump together. You might not need it all.

4. Pour the buttermilk into a small bowl and stir in 120ml (4½fl oz) of the milk, then stir this into the bowl with the flour mixture until the dough just comes together. Add more milk, if needed, to make a mixture that has the consistency of sloppy porridge that falls easily from your hand. Do not over-mix.

5. Tip the mixture into the prepared tin and smooth the top using the back of the spoon.

6. Scatter a few seeds on top and bake for 1¼ hours or until firm to the touch. Leave to cool in the tin on a wire rack for 5 minutes, then tip it out of the tin and leave it on the rack to cool completely.

Basic Recipes and Techniques

Shortcrust pastry

One of the stalwarts of classic cooking techniques, shortcrust pastry is used for making pies and tarts. Being able to make your own opens up endless possibilities. Once you feel confident with this recipe, you can up the butter to 125g (4½oz), for an even shorter (crumbly) pastry.

Makes about 325g (11½oz)

200g (7oz) plain flour
salt
100g (3½oz) chilled butter, cubed
½–1 egg, beaten

1. Sift the flour and a pinch of salt into a large bowl and add the butter. Rub the butter into the dry ingredients using your fingertips until the mixture resembles coarse breadcrumbs, or mix together using a food processor.

2. Add half the egg and stir with a fork or continue to whizz for a few seconds until the mixture looks as though it might just come together when pressed. (Prolonged processing will toughen the pastry, so don't whizz it up to the point where it forms a ball of dough.) You might need to add a little more egg, but not too much, as the mixture should be just moist enough to come together. Reserve any leftover egg to use for glazing.

3. Flatten out the dough until it is about 2cm (¾in) thick, then wrap it in cling film or a plastic bag and put in the fridge to chill for at least 30 minutes or, if you are pushed for time, in the freezer for 10–15 minutes.

Sweet shortcrust pastry

A sweet tart is one of my favourite ways to end a meal, and nothing beats a sweetened short, buttery pastry base. Shortcrust pastry must be baked blind if filled with a custard or runny filling to prevent a soggy base – see page 236 for how to do this. As with the savoury shortcrust, once you feel confident with this recipe, you can up the butter to 125g (4½oz), for an even shorter (crumbly) pastry.

Makes enough to line a 23cm (9in) tart tin

200g (7oz) plain flour
1 tbsp icing sugar
100g (3½oz) butter, chilled
   and cubed
½–1 egg, lightly beaten
salt

1. Sift the flour, a pinch of salt and the icing sugar into a large bowl and add the butter. Rub the butter into the dry ingredients using your fingertips until the mixture resembles coarse breadcrumbs, or mix together using a food processor.

2. Add half the egg and stir with a fork or continue to whizz for a few seconds until the mixture looks as though it might just come together when pressed. (Prolonged processing will toughen the pastry, so don't whizz it up to the point where it forms a ball of dough.) You might need to add a little more egg, but not too much, as the mixture should be just moist enough to come together. Reserve any leftover egg to use for glazing.

3. Flatten out the dough until it is about 2cm (¾in) thick, then wrap it in cling film or a plastic bag and put in the fridge to chill for at least 30 minutes or, if you are pushed for time, in the freezer for 10–15 minutes.

lining a tart tin and baking blind

People sometimes think that lining a tart tin with pastry is a difficult technique, but once you have it mastered it makes tart-baking a pleasure. Although you can roll out your pastry on a floured worktop, I prefer to roll it between sheets of cling film to make lining the tin simpler. Baking pastry blind is an important step, particularly for custard-filled tarts (which can be either sweet or savoury) as it will prevent a soggy and heavy base.

1. Put the pastry between 2 sheets of cling film (each larger in size than the tart tin). Using a rolling pin, roll the pastry out to no thicker than 5mm (¼in). Make sure to keep it in a round shape as well as large enough to line both the base and the side of the tin.

2. Remove the top layer of cling film, slide your hand, palm upwards, under the bottom layer of cling film, then flip the pastry over (so that the cling film is now on top) and carefully lower it into the tart tin. Press the pastry into the edges of the tin (with the cling film still attached) and, using your thumb, press the pastry along the edge of the tin to cut it for a neat finish. Remove the cling film, prick over the base with a fork and chill the pastry in the fridge for 30 minutes or in the freezer for 10 minutes (it will keep for 6 weeks, covered, in the freezer).

3. While the pastry is chilling, preheat the oven to 180°C (350°F), Gas mark 4. Line the pastry shell with baking parchment, leaving plenty to come over the side. Fill with baking beans or dried pulses (all of which can be reused repeatedly), then put in the oven and bake blind for 20–25 minutes until the pastry feels dry on the base.

4. Take out the baking beans and paper, brush the base of the pastry with the leftover beaten egg from making the pastry, then bake for another 3 minutes or until lightly golden and glazed on the base (this will prevent the filling soaking into the pastry). Set aside while you make your filling.

Puff pastry

Although puff pastry takes a little more time and effort to perfect, it's worth having a go and the results are so delicious. If you're pressed for time, you can buy puff pastry from supermarkets – although look for one that contains butter and no oils. This recipe makes generous quantities, so you can store any leftover pastry in the fridge for 48 hours or in the freezer for up to 3 months. I only include the lemon juice if making the pastry ahead, because if storing in the fridge or the freezer, it helps to keep the pastry from discolouring. I like to use iced water so that it's really cold.

Makes about 1.1kg (2lb 6oz)

450g (1lb) strong white
   bread flour
salt
1 tbsp lemon juice
200–270ml (7–9½fl oz)
   iced water (the amount of
   water will depend on the
   absorbency of the flour)
450g (1lb) chilled butter,
   still in its wrapper

baking sheet; pastry brush

1. Sift the flour and a pinch of salt into a large bowl. Mix the lemon juice with 200ml (7fl oz) of the water, pour into the flour and, using your hands, mix to a soft but not sticky dough, adding more water if necessary. This dough is called détrempe (a mixture of flour and water). It should be a slightly soft dough but not wet and sticky. Flatten it slightly, then cover it with a plastic bag, cling film or baking parchment and leave it to rest in the fridge on a baking sheet (which aids the chilling process) for 30 minutes.

2. Roll the détrempe into a rectangle about 1cm (½in) thick, then roll out the top and bottom ends and then the sides to form a shape that almost resembles a cross. The reason that you do this is so that when you place the slab of butter in the centre of the détrempe and wrap it up, there won't be too much détrempe on the top.

3. Remove the butter from the fridge, still in its wrapper and, using a rolling pin, bash it until it forms a 20 x 15cm (8 x 6in) slab about 1.5cm (⅝in) thick. Remove the wrapper, put the butter in the centre of the dough 'cross' and fold the dough over the edges of the butter to make a neat parcel, covering the butter.

4. Turn the dough over. Dust the work surface with flour to stop the dough sticking, and roll it gently out into a 40 x 20cm (16 x 8in) rectangle. Position it so that one narrow end is facing you. At the start of each rolling I like to use the 'rib-rolling' method where you press the rolling pin on to the pastry at approximately 3cm (1¼in) intervals so that it resembles ribs. I find that this method helps to distribute the butter evenly through the pastry.

5. Brush off the excess flour with a pastry brush, then fold neatly into three by lifting the end furthest away from you and putting it on the rectangle, so that only one-third of the pastry is left uncovered. Aligning the sides as accurately as possible, fold the other end over the top. Seal the edges with your hands or a rolling pin.

6. Give the dough a one-quarter turn anticlockwise, so the edges are running vertically in front of you, like a closed book. Roll out away from you, again into a rectangle to roughly the same measurements as before, brush off any excess flour and fold in three again. Seal the edges, cover with cling film or baking parchment and leave to rest in the fridge for 30 minutes.

7. Repeat the rolling, folding and resting twice more (always ensuring you start the process with the edges in the pastry running vertically, like a closed book), so that in the end the dough has been rolled out six times and has rested in the fridge three times for at least 30 minutes each time. Chill for at least 1 hour before using.

Choux pastry

Think of all the home-made profiteroles, éclairs and gougères we would miss out on if we couldn't make choux pastry. One of the things that I love about choux pastry, apart from its versatility to be both sweet and savoury, is that a little goes a long way: with just one quantity of this choux recipe you can make dozens of treats.

Makes about 325g (11½oz)

100g (3½oz) strong white
   bread flour
salt
75g (2½oz) (3oz) butter
3 eggs, beaten, or more if
   needed

1. Sift the flour and a pinch of salt into a bowl and set aside. Pour 150ml (5fl oz) water into a saucepan over a medium-high heat and add the butter. Heat, stirring, until the butter melts. Allow the mixture to come to a rolling boil, then immediately remove the pan from the heat.

2. Add the flour in one go, and beat very well with a wooden spoon until the mixture comes together with no lumps. Reduce the heat to medium and return the pan to the heat, then cook for 1 minute, stirring, until the mixture starts to fur (it slightly sticks to the base of the pan). Remove from the heat and leave it to cool for 1 minute.

3. Pour one-quarter of the beaten eggs into the pan and, using the wooden spoon, beat very well. Add a little more egg, and beat well again until the mixture comes back together.

4. Continue to add the egg, beating vigorously all the time, until the mixture has softened, is nice and shiny and has a dropping consistency. You may not need to add all the egg, or you may even need a little extra, depending on the size of the eggs. If the mixture is too stiff (because there is not enough egg), the choux pastries will be too heavy, but if the mixture is too wet (because it has too much egg), they will not hold their shape when spooned on to the baking parchment and will collapse in the oven.

5. Although the pastry is best used right away, it can be put in a bowl, covered and chilled for up to 24 hours until ready to use.

Classic brioche

If ever there was a reason to be grateful for modern appliances, it's for making brioche! What was once an arduous process for those unfortunates labouring in Marie Antoinette's kitchens is now pretty simple: leave the mixer to do all the hard work, occasionally tossing in a bit of butter with one hand while holding your glass of wine with the other.

Makes about 1kg (2lb 3oz)/3 loaves

50g (1¾oz) caster sugar
75ml (2¼fl oz) warm water
25g (1oz) fresh yeast or 15g (½oz) active dried yeast, or 1 x 7g sachets fast-action yeast
4 eggs, beaten
450g (1lb) strong white bread flour, plus extra for dusting
1 tsp salt
225g (8oz) butter, softened and cubed, plus melted butter for brushing
1 egg, beaten

three 900g (2lb) loaf tins

1. Put the sugar in a large bowl and mix with the warm water and yeast, then leave to stand for 5 minutes until creamy if using fresh or active dried yeast. If using fast-action yeast, there is no need to leave the mixture to stand.

2. Add the beaten eggs to the yeast mixture. Sift the flour and salt into the bowl of an electric mixer and add the wet ingredients, then mix to a stiff dough with the paddle.

3. When the mixture is smooth, switch to the dough hook and put on to medium speed, adding the cubes of butter a few at a time. Continue to knead in the machine for 30 minutes. The finished dough should look silky on the outside and be coming away from the sides of the bowl.

4. Cover the bowl with cling film or a plastic bag and leave it overnight in the fridge, where the dough will double in size.

5. The following day, brush the loaf tins with melted butter and dust them with flour or line them with baking parchment. Remove the dough from the fridge and knock it back in the bowl by folding it in on itself. It is crucial to work quickly at this stage, otherwise the butter will begin to melt and the dough will become too sticky to handle.

6. Divide the dough into 350g (12oz) pieces and put them into the prepared loaf tins. Brush the top of each loaf with the beaten egg. Leave the brioches to rise in a warm place in the kitchen for 45 minutes–1 hour until they have doubled in size. Preheat the oven to 180°C (350°F) Gas mark 4.

7. Gently brush the loaves with egg once more. Bake for 45–50 minutes until puffed and a rich golden brown. The loaves should sound almost hollow when tapped on the base after being removed from the tins. Turn out of the tins and leave on a wire rack to cool completely.

Crème pâtissière

One of the classic French custards, crème pâtissière is divine in everything from cakes and pastries to tarts and doughnuts.

Makes about 500g (1lb 2oz)

4 egg yolks
100g (3½oz) caster sugar
25g (1oz) plain flour
350ml (12fl oz) milk
1 tsp vanilla extract

1. In a bowl, whisk the egg yolks with the sugar until light and thick, then sift in the flour and whisk to combine.

2. Heat the milk in a saucepan over a medium heat and bring it slowly just up to the boil. Pour the milk over the egg mixture, whisking constantly.

3. Return the mixture to the pan and stir over a medium-low heat until it comes to a gentle boil (it must boil for it to thicken). Continue to cook, stirring or whisking constantly for 2 minutes or until it has thickened to ensure that there are no lumps.

4. Remove the pan from the heat, add the vanilla extract and immediately pour it into a bowl, to stop it cooking further.

5. Cover with cling film and leave to cool. This will prevent a skin from forming. When completely cool, put it in the fridge until needed.

Classic buttercream icing

A rich addition to cakes, buns and cupcakes, buttercream is a traditional and versatile coating and filling that can be adapted by adding a variety of flavourings.

Makes 675g

225g (8oz) butter
450g (1lb) icing sugar
1 tsp vanilla extract

1. Using a wooden spoon or an electric beater, beat the butter until soft. Sift in the icing sugar gradually and beat well after each addition. Add the vanilla extract and 2 tablespoons hot water, then mix together thoroughly.

Variations:

For Chocolate buttercream Substitute 50g (1¾oz) sifted cocoa powder for 50g (1¾oz) of the icing sugar.

For Orange, lemon or lime buttercream Substitute a fruit juice of your choice for the hot water and add the zest of your chosen fruit.

For Caramel buttercream Dissolve 200g (7oz) granulated sugar in a saucepan with 110ml (4fl oz) cold water over a gentle heat. Stir until all the sugar has dissolved, then remove the spoon and continue to simmer until the syrup caramelises to a chestnut colour, add 110ml (4fl oz) cold water, but do not stir again – be careful at this stage, when you add the water, the mixture will bubble up. Remove from the heat and leave to cool. Stir until the sauce is a smooth consistency. Once cooled, add 4 tablespoons of this caramel sauce to the buttercream and mix thoroughly.

For Butterscotch buttercream Put 110g (3½oz) butter and 175g (6oz) dark soft brown sugar into a heavy-bottomed saucepan and melt gently over a low heat. Simmer for 5 minutes, then remove from the heat and gradually stir in 225ml (8fl oz) single cream and ½ teaspoon vanilla extract. Return to the heat and stir for 2–3 minutes until the sauce is absolutely smooth. Leave to cool. Once cooled, add 3 tablespoons of this butterscotch sauce to the buttercream and mix thoroughly.

Bread techniques

Kneading and rising a yeast dough are important stages of dough-making and can't be rushed. The kneading, whether by hand or machine, develops the gluten to give bread its texture and structure, whereas leaving the dough to rise sufficiently is essential for lightness and a good crumb. You can use a stand mixer for kneading, but you can also knead by hand, as explained here.

To knead bread dough by hand

Turn out the mixed ingredients on to a lightly floured work surface and knead strongly, pushing the dough away from you with the heel of your hand and then pulling it back towards you. This will take 8–10 minutes. It should be springy when you press the dough with your finger and feel smooth to the touch.

Rising bread dough

When leaving bread dough to rise, cover it with cling film to avoid it being affected by draughts, and put it in a warm part of the kitchen – but not above 36°C (96.8°F), which would kill off the yeast and halt the dough from rising – for 1–2 hours or until doubled in size. The dough has risen enough when you push it gently with a floured fingertip and it does not spring back.

Toasting nuts

Oven-toasting nuts not only makes them deliciously crunchy, but it also enhances their flavour. Don't take your eyes off them while they toast, as they seem to go from undercooked to burned in seconds!

Hazelnuts

To toast hazelnuts, spread them out on a baking tray and cook in an oven preheated to 200°C (400°F) Gas mark 6 for 7–10 minutes until the skins have darkened and the nuts are golden underneath. Wrap the nuts in a clean tea towel (it will slightly stain, so don't use your favourite one) and rub them together for a few seconds to loosen the skins. Pick the hazelnuts out from the skins.

Almonds

To toast almonds, put them in the oven and toast as above. The skins of almonds must be removed before toasting; buy blanched almonds or put almonds with skins into a pan of boiling water over a medium heat and cook for 1 minute. Take one almond out to test it by squeezing it; the almond should pop out of its skin. If ready, drain the rest of the almonds, then put them in a tea towel and rub them for a few seconds to remove the skins.

Pistachios

To toast pistachio nuts. put them in the oven preheated as above and toast them for 4–5 minutes until golden.

Index

Acknowledgements

There are so many lovely people to thank for their contributions to this book. As ever, big hugs and much love to all my wonderful family and friends for their never-ending support. A big smooch and thank you to my husband, Isaac, for being so fabulous and being beside me in everything I do. Huge hugs to my sister, Simone Michel, for the never-ending inspiration; I couldn't have done it without you.

To Susan McKeown, Rebecca Woods and Sam Head for so much brilliant help getting this book to the finishing line. To all the A-team at Ballymaloe Cookery School and at Rachel's restaurant in Cork city — thank you all for being so fabulous.

A huge thank you, as always, to the wonderful team at HarperCollins who work so hard to put my books together. To Grace Cheetham, Zoe Berville and Isabel Hayman-Brown for their never-ending patience, kindness and editorial support. To Sim and Micaela for their design expertise and beautiful art direction. To Isabel and Katie for their innovative publicity and marketing campaigns and to the super HarperCollins team in Ireland: Mary Byrne, Tony Purdue and Anne-Marie Dolan.

As always, it was such a pleasure to work with my brilliant photo-shoot team. Thank you to Maja Smend and her assistant Sam Folan, whose images are always exceptional. To Annie Rigg, whose food styling and preparation is second to none, and to Lydia Brun, whose prop-styling nous is unrivalled. A big hug and thank you to Nicky Clarke for the fabulous hair and make-up in this book and to my friend and designer Lucy Downes of Sphere One, who never fails to supply me with the most divine cashmere, wool and silk for photo shoots and life in general!

A big shout out to the brilliant Fiona, Alison and Maclean Lindsay and Roz Ellman at Limelight Management and also to Jan Cutler for all her hard work. Last but not least, to all the wonderful people who buy my books. Thank you all from the bottom of my heart.

HarperCollins*Publishers*
1 London Bridge Street
London SE1 9GF

www.harpercollins.co.uk

First published by
HarperCollins*Publishers* 2017

10 9 8 7 6 5 4 3 2 1

Text © Rachel Allen, 2017
Photography © Maja Smend, 2017
Illustrations © Micaela Alcaino, 2017
Food styling: Annie Rigg
Props styling: Lydia Brun
Hair and make-up: Nicky Clarke

Rachel Allen asserts the moral right to be
identified as the author of this work

A catalogue record of this book is available
from the British Library

ISBN 978-0-00-817982-3

Printed and bound at GPS Group

Please note

Oven temperatures are given for a standard
oven; if you are using a fan oven, reduce the
stated temperature by 20°C.

Eggs, vegetables and fruit are medium unless
otherwise stated.

In Ireland, you can buy regular fresh cream
which is almost as rich as double cream and is
suitable for recipes calling for double cream.
Bicarbonate of soda is sold as 'bread soda'.